Designing
ALBERTA
GARDENS

The Complete Guide to Beautiful Gardens

JAN MATHER

RED DEER COLLEGE PRESS

The Publishers
Red Deer College Press
56 Avenue & 32 Street Box 5005
Red Deer Alberta Canada T4N 5H5

Designed by Kunz & Associates
Printed and bound in Canada by D.W. Friesen Ltd. for Red Deer College Press

Financial support provided by the Alberta Foundation for the Arts, a beneficiary of the Lottery Fund of the Government of Alberta, the Department of Communications and Red Deer College.

DISCLAIMER: This book does not endorse any particular product, supplier, method or practice. Examples are presented for the purposes of general information only. For specific information gardeners should always refer to specific instructions from suppliers or manufacturers. The author and Red Deer College Press are not responsible for suppliers' products, instructions or services nor for any loss or injury resulting from the same.

Canadian Cataloguing in Publication Data
Mather, Jan, 1954 –
Designing Alberta gardens
Includes index.
ISBN 0-88995-111-X
1. Gardens – Alberta – Design. 2. Gardening – Alberta. I. Title.
SB472.32.C2M38 1994   712'.6   C93-091892-4

CONTENTS

AUTHOR'S ACKNOWLEDGEMENTS

This book would not have been possible without the talent and dedication of a team of professionals.

I am very grateful to the Managing Editor of Red Deer College Press, Dennis Johnson, for his enthusiastic support of this project. I also wish to extend my sincere thanks to Dennis Johnson and Carolyn Dearden for their editorial contributions and to Vicki Mix for keeping us all sane and organized.

I also wish to thank the following people for their assistance: Michael Dawe, Archivist, Red Deer and District Museum; Stephen Lyons, Canadian Pacific Archives, Montreal; Judy Wakoluk, Historian, Heritage Park, Calgary; Buck Godwin, Olds College.

Special thanks are also due Heidi Petzold and Alex Riach who contributed their delightful recipe for the Children's Garden; to my dear friend Bryon Fischer, who generously provided his research expertise and many hours of endless horticultural editing; to James Heeks and Donna Burton, who provided an extensive selection of photographs; to Dennis Johnson and John Grogan, who also supplied photographs; to all the Alberta gardeners who generously offered to have their gardens photographed; and finally, to my husband and children for their endless love and support and to my best friend for always being there—I thank you all.

INTRODUCTION

One of the many pleasures of being a garden designer is witnessing the making of a garden. During the initial consultation my client and I will tour the proposed site to discover its hidden potential. Then, together, we create a garden—always a delightful place, sometimes full of sequential blooms and brilliant colour and sometimes simply a tranquil corner with dappled shade and a garden bench.

Gardens are as different from one another as the people who create them. Each has its own unique character and mood, but beneath these differences run some basic design principles that every beautiful garden draws upon. In this book I have attempted to distill the sum of my experience as a garden designer and remove some of the mystery that surrounds the making of a garden.

Garden design is a creative adventure but one that owes much to the dedicated plantsmen and horticulturalists of the past who bequeathed us a legacy of hardy plant material. So we begin our exploration of Alberta garden design with a glance to the past and a small tribute to their pioneering efforts. Space limitations prevented including a more extensive review of historic horticultural contributions, and I offer my apologies to those omitted.

Next, we turn to the fundamentals of design and explore the qualities that breathe life into a garden plan. With a knowledge of these, we go step by step

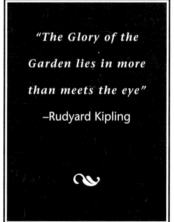

"The Glory of the Garden lies in more than meets the eye"
–Rudyard Kipling

from formulating a wish list to the analysis of your site, which results in a series of abstract bubble drawings. In turn, we create a working drawing and planting strategy, which become the map of your dream garden. Because trees and shrubs form the framework of garden design, I have included reference lists of hardy coniferous and deciduous shrubs and trees before turning to chapters on specialty gardens, which will help stimulate and refine your ideas before incorporating one or more of them into your garden design.

There are specialty gardens to capitalize on the potential of virtually all sites—delightful spring gardens, playful children's gardens, lavish cutting gardens, formal rose gardens, tranquil water gardens, ambrosial scented gardens, beguiling rock gardens, dappled shade gardens, single- and multicoloured gardens and garden accents to fit any theme. Each specialty garden chapter offers ideas and advice—from selecting a site to creative planting strategies to extensive lists of plant material suitable for the Alberta climate.

The purpose of this book is to transform your ideas into workable plans by offering you creative design strategies specifically suited to Alberta gardens. I invite you to explore your garden's potential and, with the help of this book, develop your own piece of paradise.

–JAN MATHER, FEBRUARY, 1994

ALBERTA'S HORTICULTURAL HERITAGE

"I have named a province vast,

and for its beauty famed

By thy dear name to be

hereafter known"

–Marquis of Lorne to

HRH Princess Louise

Caroline Alberta

New settlers to western Canada came from virtually all over the world, but they had in common the promise of land and the hope of taming a new frontier. At first they arrived on foot and in Red River carts, stagecoaches and riverboats. Later, with the new transcontinental railway spanning the prairies, they arrived by train, their treasured heirloom seeds tucked safely away with their dreams.

Westward migration was supported by a number of official and unofficial initiatives. Prompted by the rapid industrialization of eastern Canada and its growing demand for bread, the federal government began a vigorous campaign to lure settlers to the nation's great wheat-growing region. Indispensable to this initiative were the building of the Canadian Pacific Railway (CPR) and the discovery of an early ripening hard spring wheat. With the prospect of increasing revenues from shipping western agricultural produce east, the CPR also began offering incentives to western settlers. These official recruitment programs dovetailed neatly into an excess of unofficial and often inflated claims about the West's unlimited bounty.

Red Deer CPR Railway Garden, May, 1912

RAILWAY GARDENS

Railway gardens became the calling cards of the CPR's western settlement programs. These gardens' colourful flowers and many shrubs and trees advertised the fertility of the West. The idea began with CPR employees David Hysop and N. Stewart Dunlop in the late 1800s and was soon accepted wholeheartedly by CPR management. Station agents voluntarily started cultivating small plots of ground and planting seeds supplied by the company. Eventually, along the endless miles of steel, gardens flourished.

As the popularity of railway gardens spread, the CPR recognized the economic benefits of its volunteer beautification project. A forestry department was established to manage existing railway gardens and to turn what had been an informal activity into a formal program. By 1912 the CPR had established greenhouses to distribute hardy bedding plants such as marigolds, pansies, petunias and snapdragons, and perennials such as delphiniums, peonies and shasta daisies. But the new department faced a number of challenges: railway garden plant material had to withstand both harsh winters and a regular rain of soot from passing trains.

Undeterred, the CPR Forestry Department met these challenges and soon developed design criteria for each new railway garden. Early designs were formal, with straight lines and endless symmetry, and appealed to visitors, who enjoyed viewing colourful flower gardens artfully arranged.

Not everyone, however, advocated early railway garden design. Critics complained that formal designs didn't reflect natural surroundings, that shrubs and trees weren't grouped in picturesque compositions and that picket fences often obstructed views from trains. The CPR responded with a reevaluation of design principles, and some gardens took on a decidedly different look. In Alberta, for example, station gardens at Fort Macleod and Red Deer were designed to be natural and parklike. Fort Macleod citizens took pride in an attractive circular garden, a combination of natural and formal plantings around a bandstand. The Red Deer station kept a colourful garden abounding with annuals and perennials informally arranged around an elaborate fountain basin. Cheerful daisies and annual alyssum bordered the pathway around the basin, providing a welcome relief from dusty travel.

For many years representatives of the Forestry Department travelled across the West, inspecting gardens and offering suggestions and improvements. They measured the value of a flower garden by the pleasure it provided to visitors and by the contentedness and peace of mind it gave the station agents and surrounding community. As the editor of the *Canadian Municipal Journal* reflected, "The man with a nice garden is a decent industrious man, who will bring up his children to be the best kind of citizens."

Because western railway stations were often the hub of small towns, representing their only link with the outside world, Department employees soon found themselves dispensing valuable horticultural information to entire communities. But their civic service did not end there. As their skills developed they became active in establishing horticultural societies and instrumental in developing policies for town improvements. Garden club activities of today have their roots in the annual bench shows, garden tours, plant sales, demonstrations and public services first promoted and offered by railway gardeners.

The success of CPR railway gardens prompted other railways to imitate them, which is, of course, the highest form of flattery. With both the Canadian National and the Grand Trunk railways developing similar gardens, competition extended beyond pure commerce to the beauty of their stations.

Changing times, however, brought significant changes to railway gardens. With the outbreak of World War I, ornamental sites were ploughed under in order to grow potatoes and mixed vegetables. After the War, the CPR appointed floral committees to modernize the gardens and reduce material and labour costs. They discouraged traditional formal designs and urged more natural permanent plantings.

Despite scaled-down resources and intense promotion of these design changes, the charming geometric railway garden of the 19th century lived on. In fact it thrived under the direction of Chief Horticulturalist J.R. Almey from 1929 to 1960. Perhaps pioneers' dreams of taming the new West influenced their desire for structure in the garden. Perhaps the CPR's international reputation for beautifying the prairie provinces made accepting design changes difficult. Its gardens were, after all, acclaimed as some of the most beautiful in the world.

Today, the romantic era of railway gardens has virtually disappeared beneath the broad surfaces of concrete parking lots. However, no one can deny the legacy passed down to modern gardeners in Alberta and across the West. Lovers of gardens will be pleased to note that railway stations are again including gardening designs in their remodelling plans. Perhaps railway gardens will bloom again across the prairies as a satisfying reminder of our links to the past.

EXPERIMENTAL FARMS

The dreams of new settlers may have been founded on their desire for rich soil and a prosperous living, but it was hard labour and resourcefulness that spurred real growth in the West. Early settlers faced many disappointments, including the loss of their heirloom seeds to the ravaging winds and extreme shifts in temperature that characterized the prairie climate. The demand for hardy plant material soared as pioneers struggled to make a living from the dry prairie soil and to protect their properties from the elements. Determined to improve their surroundings, a few began using native plant material. Their successes, in turn, encouraged researchers at experimental farms.

Recognizing settlers' needs, the federal government, at the turn of the century, launched a program to distribute hardy plant species in the form of free seedlings for shelterbelt plantings. Conditions governing their distribution included directions on proper soil preparation, spacing of trees, cultivation of soil, fencing guidelines and a system of inspection.

In Alberta, horticultural research occurred at federal experimental farms at Beaverlodge, Lacombe and Lethbridge, at Brooks Horticultural Station and at colleges and universities. With these programs in place, shelterbelts and gardens soon began flourishing across the province.

The work of visionary and dedicated plantsmen and pioneers is seen today in Alberta gardens. Their efforts have resulted in a landscape coloured with golden grasses, shrubs that flower and bear fruit, trees that both shelter and decorate, and flowers that bring great pleasure.

GARDEN DESIGN BASICS

"The great challenge for the garden designer is not to make the garden look natural, but to make the garden so that the people in it will feel natural"

–Lawrence Halprin

Garden design is the artful arrangement of plants and structures. It is the creative combination of colour, texture and form within balanced, rhythmic and proportionate designs. A successful garden—one that delights all the senses and reflects your personality—begins with a plan that best fulfills your garden dreams and your garden's potential.

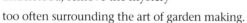

Take a moment to recall a memorable garden scene. Perhaps you saw it through the gate of a neighbour's coveted backyard or in a glossy magazine. The visual impact of this scene, its inherent beauty and character, results from the subtle combination of design elements that, when understood, remove the mystery too often surrounding the art of garden making.

The purpose of gardens is pleasure. Here, a quiet retreat is ideally located for enjoying a spring display.

Garden making is not a complex art form reserved for specialists. It's for everyone. The purpose of this guide to garden planning is to make the process simple. We begin with a look at basic design elements and move through five essential steps to garden planning. Whether you are remodelling an existing garden in Wainwright or establishing a brand new landscape in Innisfail, the steps for successful garden design remain the same, and once you take them you'll discover that you're closer to the garden of your dreams than you would have believed possible.

THE BASIC ELEMENTS OF GARDEN DESIGN

Today you can choose from traditional or contemporary gardening styles, and you can tailor them to create a piece of paradise for yourself. Whatever your likes and creative abilities, pleasurable outdoor living space is possible—in spite of adverse growing conditions, skeptical neighbours, stray dogs, cats and kids, and an annual resolution to minimize spending. The process of successful garden design begins with identifying the basic elements that enable you to analyze the different qualities you admire most in gardens and to incorporate them into your new garden plan.

Style

To start this creative adventure we must first define the word *style*. Different garden design styles evoke different feelings or responses. Styles are expressions of personal taste, but they tend to be formal or informal based upon the dominant pattern or arrangement of lines within a design.

Curved lines soften the harsh edges of permanent structures and gently lead the viewer's eye through the garden. Strong flowing lines, not meaningless serpentine wiggles, will move leisurely and informally from one area to another to create a natural sweeping effect.

Straight lines reinforce the architectural lines of buildings and create a strong sense of direction. A formal garden may contain, for example, rectangular shrub beds and straight sidewalks along the foundation. Provided that the planting arrangement is interesting and well balanced, the straight lines of such a garden will give viewers a sense of permanence and strength.

Angles provide visual contrasts in both formal and informal settings, and establish focal points to guide the viewer's eye. Imagine, for instance, a vine-clad octagonal gazebo at the end of a winding garden path. Here, flowing lines lead the eye to the visually contrasting element. For angles to be successfully incorporated into the garden, they should stay within the same angle family: 30–60–90° and 45–90–180°. Otherwise the result is chaotic.

Working with Your Surroundings

The process of garden making continues by heeding the advice of Alexander Pope, an eighteenth-century poet, who advised us to respect the "genius of the place." This means being attentive to what exists in a given area and shaping ideas about line in relation to it. If, for example, your house is a ranch-style bungalow on an acreage surrounded by rolling hills

The straight lines of formal gardens create a strong sense of purpose.

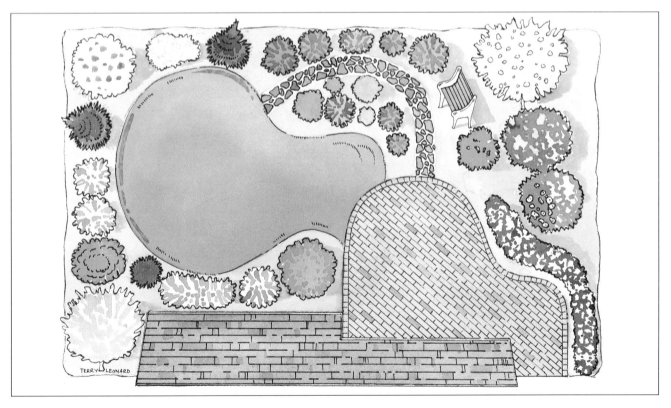

The flowing lines of informal gardens produce a casual effect.

and native stands of trees, you would avoid creating a billiard table-smooth lawn. Instead you might consider contouring or reshaping the elevations immediately around the bungalow and planting large groupings of similar species in strong sweeping lines. This balances the visual perspective and gives the house a sense of belonging in the landscape. Conversely, if your house is a narrow two-storey on a rectangular city lot with overgrown trees, some selective pruning may allow you to soften the straight lines and develop a low-growing shade garden. Or a small slope may inspire a colourful rock garden. A little imagination combined with what you have available can create many exciting possibilities.

Choosing a style that makes the most of its surroundings is a first step in designing a beautiful garden, but it must be followed by steps that ensure that the plants and structures exist in harmonious relation to each other.

Balance

Balance, the next step, controls the even distribution of shapes, sizes, textures and colours. We see it in terms of visual emphasis or weight. For example, an informal curved bed with six potentilla in a straight row will result in an unbalanced look. This can be improved by softening the arrangement into small groupings of plants and shrubs of varying heights and colours. A more effective arrangement might include one dwarf pine, three dwarf cranberries and two potentilla.

Strictly speaking, *formal balance* is symmetrical: one side of a central axis mirrors the other. Such a pattern gives a comfortable impression of perma-

Symmetrical balance (top) occurs when one side of a central axis mirrors the other, creating a sense of order and intention. Asymmetrical balance (bottom) places unequal amounts and types of plant material on either side of a central axis to occasion a more informal look.

This informal arrangement relies on repeated groupings of plant material to create a gentle sweeping rhythm.

nence and distinct intention. When a sidewalk cuts a front yard in two, you can create symmetrical balance by placing the same arrangement of plants in reverse order on opposite sides.

In modern practice, we rarely create the rigidly geometric formal designs of the past. But we can add variety and interest to an informal design by focusing attention on, say, a small formal rose garden. Or we can do the opposite: focus attention on a small informal perennial bed within a more formal setting.

Asymmetrical balance is informal and relies on visual emphasis as opposed to reflection. For example, you may have unequal amounts of plant material on either side of a central axis, while still maintaining the overall even distribution of shapes, sizes, textures and colours. Without balance of some kind, the scene is either monotonous or chaotic.

The same visual emphasis that is applied to the distribution of plant material is also applied to structures. Close your eyes and envision a vine-covered pergola in the back right-hand corner of your yard with nothing else around it. Now try the same scene again, but include a few trees and shrubs and perhaps a wooden trellis or bench on the left side. The result is a balanced garden composition.

Rhythm

Rhythm is a regularly recurring accent or beat. In design it is achieved by the repeated use of certain elements, such as colour, form, texture and line pattern. Like the familiar rhythm of a song, the musical beat of a design provides continuity and a sense of structure. An enjoyable rhythm contains only enough variety to be interesting. How much variety is necessary depends upon your tastes and the intent of the design, but the expression "less is more" has considerable merit. Rather than planting twenty different shrubs in one particular bed, group two, three and five of the same variety. The rhythm of such a sequence will hold more interest and strengthen the overall design without overwhelming the scene.

Proportion

Proportion refers to the comparative value, or size, of two quantities within a given composition. For example, when a large overbearing tree is planted in the front garden of a small house, the tree commands too much attention, distracting the eye from the main feature—the house. A dwarf tree variety and a large house will have the same effect—the small tree commands too much attention because it is not in proportion to the size of the house. Houses in new neighbourhoods often create this effect because there aren't any mature trees to create a sense of proportion. When planning a flower bed, shrub bed, patio or deck, be sure the size is in relation to the house and surrounding area. And remember that proper balance, rhythm and proportion will create harmony and unity, the ultimate goals in garden design.

Colour

Colour, texture and form are the qualities that breathe life into harmonious garden compositions. Each trait can be manipulated to create an expression of personal taste.

Plant material that isn't in proportion to its surroundings will draw attention to itself and away from the overall design intention. To avoid the disproportion shown in these designs, always consider the mature size of your selections.

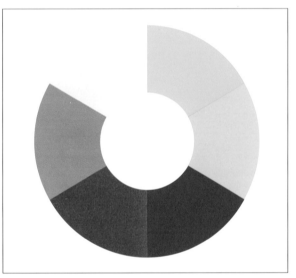

Use the colour wheel to determine analogous and complementary colour schemes.

Colour in the garden evokes the greatest response. Although colours are neither hot nor cold in a physical sense, they can impart feelings of warmth or coolness. Some gardeners prefer bright carnival colours like blazing reds and golden yellows to complement their homes, while others pick gentle soothing combinations of pastel pinks, mauves, blues and purples. Still others prefer a monochromatic scheme, such as a serene white garden with green foliage as a solitary companion colour.

We see colour when light waves of specific lengths are reflected or absorbed by pigments. For example, the fiery red geranium appears red because its pigment absorbs all wavelengths except red. The green of its foliage, produced by chlorophyll, absorbs all light waves except green. Tranquil white gardens, however, appear white not because of pigmentation, but because of tiny air spaces in the tissues that refract and reflect all light waves. The strength of colours will be affected by the intensity of sunlight. That is why the colour palette of your garden will appear dull and muted on a cloudy day and vivid and clear on a sunny day.

Like an artist weaving colours into a tapestry, you can create painterly compositions based on a few simple guidelines having to do with the interrelationships of colours and the effects and moods created by different colour combinations. Choosing a colour scheme for your garden is purely a personal affair. No rule book governs the colour arrangements you choose, but the connection between your garden and the interior and exterior of your house will be reinforced if you select from a common range of colours. The predominant colour theme is usually influenced by the colour of your house, especially the exterior: your choices for colour in the garden should complement rather than distract.

To help you make suitable choices within acceptable colour ranges, you should consult a colour wheel, which shows the basic interrelationships of colours. Any three adjoining colours are said to be *analogous*. Warm colours, such as red, red-orange, orange, yellow-orange and yellow, tend to make plants appear closer. To illustrate this sensory phenomenon in the flower bed, imagine brilliant yellow and orange marigolds and calendulas planted next to orange lilies and blanketflowers. These colours will not only provide a salsa-hot display but will bring a distant part of the yard into sharp focus. In a deep narrow lot, you can use this effect with yellow flowering shrubs at the three-quarter-way mark to create the illusion of a smaller space.

The rich autumn colour of a mountain ash complements clear blue skies.

Choose shrubs and trees that offer four-season interest. A colourful amur maple can offer stunning contrast against mature spruce trees.

Generally, cool colours, such as green, blue-green, blue, blue-violet and violet, recede or appear farther away. A planting of tall sky-blue delphiniums in the back corner of your garden will make the garden seem larger. On the other hand, blue also evokes feelings of tranquillity, so cool refreshing blue bellflowers, purple alyssum or a carpet of forget-me-nots are perfect for closeup viewing beside a patio or bordering a garden path. And the sweet scent of alyssum is a delight in itself.

Colours opposite each other on the colour wheel are *complementary*—yellow/violet, orange/blue and red/green are examples. These contrasting colours are powerful and vibrant combinations. Imagine clear blue delphiniums next to orange marigolds or a tawny orange daylily beside mauve-blue phlox—perfect for the eclectic gardener but a bit startling for most. Plants with silver or grey foliage, such as 'Silver Mound' artemisia or grey lavender cotton, can serve as peacemakers among these bold colour combinations and can play an invaluable role in evening gardens. The annual dusty miller also complements many brightly contrasting flowers.

In planning your colour scheme, consider not only flower colours but their bloom times. You can select early, mid- and late-season blooms from an enormous variety of annuals and perennials. With careful planning, you can create a succession of colourful blooms throughout the season. Remember that flowering times for many plants vary throughout the province. Local garden centres and horticultural societies should be your source of best advice.

Colour in the garden is not restricted to just flowers. Take a close look at shrubs and trees, and examine the many other, often subtler, instances of colour. Foliage, stems, fruit, seeds and bark all contribute variety and contrast. The greenery that shrubs and trees provide, for example, can serve as a background for flowering plants while offering interest in themselves.

Texture

Texture adds special visual interest to the garden. Texture refers to the roughness or smoothness, coarseness or fineness of plants, flowers or foliage. For example, the large cabbagelike leaves of bergenia have a very different quality than the finely textured leaves of grass pinks and therefore create different effects. One appears large and indelicate; the other appears graceful and airy.

The appearance of texture is also affected by the interaction of light and shade, which creates different optical effects. Larger-leaved bergenias will appear closer because their leaf surface is dense and reflects light, making them ideal background plants. On the other hand, the smaller leaves of grass pinks appear farther away because more light filters through their foliage, making them better suited to foreground plantings.

Texture, however, is not just a quality of plants. Other materials will also produce a variety of textural effects in your garden. Coarsely textured uncut field stones, for example, have a rugged informal appeal and might be suitable for a lightly used garden path, but they would be a poor choice for a heavy traffic area. Generally speaking, too many different textures in one setting create a chaotic effect.

Form

Form refers to the general shape or outline of plants, trees, shrubs and structures. Plant material can take many shapes or forms. Shrubs, trees and flowers can be round, columnar, vase-shaped, pyramidal,

Nuances of light can have a dramatic on how we see texture. The contrasting textures of this mature fruit tree's airy canopy and the hedge's dense growth are intensified by sunlight.

The upright form and summer fruit of this highbush cranberry add interest to an inviting pathway.

oval—the list is daunting. They can also grow vertically or spread horizontally. Whether they are short and squat or tall and narrow, their three-dimensional mass determines their scale. For example, the pendulous form of the cutleaf weeping birch leads the eye back to the ground; the ascending form of evergreens leads the eye upward, giving a sense of height. Horizontal forms emphasize lateral space and soften the transition between smaller shrubs and soil. Intricate forms tend to provoke curiosity and interest, and when suitably located they can gently coax the visitor to explore the garden further.

Different shapes provide interest and variety. However, rhythm through repetition will help unify your design. If you choose a patio with curved soft lines, the theme can be echoed, for instance, in companions of roundish shrubs of varying sizes.

This brief glimpse at the interrelationships between balance, rhythm and proportion, and colour, form and texture can spark any number of creative garden design ideas that will harmonize with your surroundings and complement your home. Now, with the basics in mind and a fresh cup of tea, we can begin the design process.

STEPS TO GARDEN PLANNING

"As is the gardener, so is the garden"

–Thomas Fuller

STEP 1

What makes a garden delightful is the unique interaction of plants and people. For some, delight is found in a garden bench tucked beneath the arching branches of a flowering crabapple or lilac tree, a private place of rest and repose. For others, delight is found in a small corner of a lot with a single shrub rose and a few perennials. But making a garden a delightful place requires some imagination and planning before the work of planting begins. This chapter will help you discover your yard's potential and help you to design a garden that is both practical and artful.

Don't overlook the decorative potential of garages and storage sheds. Add sun-worshipping annuals to provide dazzling summer colour.

As you proceed through the following five steps to garden planning, you will undoubtedly come up with many ideas and possibilities—some workable, some not—and that is as it should be. Tinkering with ideas is an important part of the creative process.

STEP ONE:

CREATING A WISH LIST

Your wish list should embrace ideas and possibilities for the garden of your dreams. Ideas for designs will come from a variety of sources: studying magazines and books, collecting pictures of favourite gardens and their embellishments, visiting your favourite garden centre or joining a garden club or society. Return that rototiller you borrowed from your neigh-

With a fresh coat of paint and a cheerful window box, storage sheds can add charm to any garden.

bour last autumn and hint that you'd enjoy seeing the garden. Gardeners are among the most gracious of hosts (unless they have just returned from holidays and the teenager they hired for maintenance forgot to water) and will likely be glad to share their advice and enthusiasm. At the very least, check if any of your potential plans will conflict with your neighbour's interests.

With pictures and ideas in mind about what delights you, sit down with your family and work through the accompanying Wish List. This task will provide a careful assessment of the needs of the family members who will use the garden. No doubt, as in all family discussions, certain compromises will be in order. Keep in mind that the more input each family member has into the garden plan, the more rewarding the completed project will be. Remember, too, that gardening is a continual experiment—allow for change as skills develop and your children grow. On occasion you may discover that within the once-a-week lawn-mowing champion lurks a gardener keen to trade his or her noisy machine for a quiet hoe.

The following Wish List contains a number of potential questions you should ask yourself and your family as you begin the garden design process. Add or delete items to suit your needs.

Wish List

Garden maintenance...

Minimum?

Moderate?

High?

Special interests...

Annuals?

Perennials?

Fruit trees?

Shrubs?

Vines?

Herbs?

Vegetables?

Flower colours?

Spring gardens?

Children's gardens?

Cutting gardens?

Rose gardens?

Water gardens?

Scented gardens?

Rock gardens?

Shade gardens?

Colour gardens?

Wildflowers?

Containers?

Foliage?

Wildlife?

Garden accents—statuary

or other ornaments?

Garden styles...

Formal?

Informal?

Straight lines?

Curved lines?

Borders?

Island beds?

Other?

Entertainment needs...

Small groups?

Large groups?

Tables and seating?

Deck?

Patio?

Gazebo?

Pergola?

Hot tub?

Outdoor cooking...

Barbeque?

Fire pit?

Surface materials...

Brick?

Concrete?

Wood?

Other?

Lawn games...

Badminton?

Croquet?

Horseshoes?

Putting green?

Tennis?

Other?

Views from your

property...

Good views to take

advantage of?

Unsightly views to hide?

Privacy screening from

street or neighbours?

Service areas...

Garage?

Greenhouse?

Potting shed?

Storage shed?

Dog run?

Clothesline?

Compost bins?

Garbage containers?

Children's play areas...

Play space size?

Playhouse?

Sandbox?

Swings and slide?

Climber?

Budget...

Limited?

Moderate?

High?

Other considerations...

Family members' allergies?

Family members' special

needs? (wheelchair access?)

Automatic watering?

Night lighting?

STEP TWO: ANALYZING THE SITE
Drawing the Base Plan

Whether you are renovating a small corner of your backyard or starting a brand new landscape, analyzing your site will determine its dimensions and bring to your attention factors that will influence your plant selections. It includes surveying in detail existing topography, plant material and permanent structures, and how each affects the microclimate of your site. Shadows, wind patterns, temperatures, relative humidity and views from various places, both indoors and out, are also evaluated. From this information, you develop a base plan, an accurate map representing the physical features of your property.

To begin, you need paper, pencil and a measuring tape of approximately 15 M (50'). With these in hand, go outside and begin measuring and commenting on everything on your property using the following points as guides. Remember, at this stage your measurements should be accurate, but don't worry if your drawing is sketchy. The base plan will be redrawn indoors later.

1. Begin by orienting your site on paper with a base line. A base line can be the back wall of your house if you are designing only for the backyard. Note the outside dimensions of the property if a total yard design is to be completed. If you are redesigning a small area, then just those measurements are necessary. If your site is out in an open field and no base line is available, improvise with two stakes and some string. Standard practice is to draw the plan with north at the top or left side of the paper.

2. Note the topography and natural features of the property. Is there a slope that will require retaining walls or special plantings? Are there existing or potential drainage problems? Check again after a heavy rain for water pooling. Are there noises from a nearby road that need buffering?

3. Locate the house, driveway and garage within the property lines. Be sure to include easements, power boxes and fire hydrants. Include all windows, doors, downspouts, hose connections, gas meters and overhead utility lines. If the prospect of substantial digging exists, it will be necessary to mark all underground utility lines. Call all your local utility companies including cable, natural gas and electrical.

4. Locate the storage shed, if you have one, on the base plan. Is it in a suitable place? Does it need to be moved or screened with vines or shrubs? Can its appearance be improved with window boxes?

5. Locate existing fences, patios, decks, gazebos and pathways. Do some of these need improving?

6. Note the spread of existing shrubs and trees.

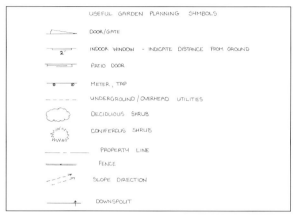

These garden planning symbols will assist you in labelling your designs.

Determining Percentage of Slope

To determine the percentage of slope on your site, you'll need a carpenter's line level, enough string to run the length of your yard and two stakes. Stake one end of the string at ground level where the slope begins. Run the string down the yard to the base of the slope. Hang the line level from the string and stake the loose string end at the level height. Measure the distance from the string to the ground at the base of the slope. Divide this amount by the distance between the two stakes at ground level to get the percentage of slope. If the slope is excessive (greater than 10%) you may want to consider having the area professionally terraced to make maintenance easier and provide better growing conditions for shrubs and trees.

Give the dimensions of the tree canopy or branch spread as well as the diameter of the trunk. Do some shrubs or trees need to be removed or pruned? Could the removal of a few select branches change dense shade to dappled, allowing for a small shade garden?

7. Note any existing flower beds. Are they in appropriate locations? Are they the styles of beds you want?

8. Note both scenic and unsightly views. Can scenic views be improved with selective tree removal or pruning? Can unsightly views be screened with trees or vine-clad trellises?

9. Note the views from indoors. Do you want to see the children's play area from the kitchen window or view a potential rose garden from the dining room window?

10. Note local bylaws and possible restrictions in your area. (Certain municipalities have architectural limitations regarding the selection of plant material and codes regarding fences, fire pits, gazebos and the like. For example, certain trees might be designated heritage trees and cannot, therefore, be removed.)

Once you've completed your site analysis, you're ready to refine your outdoor sketches into a scaled base plan. Redrawing the base plan requires a few basic drawing instruments: graph paper, circle and triangle templates, soft lead pencil, scaled ruler and tracing paper. These are all available at most stationery or art supply stores. Graph paper (available in sheets or rolls) must be lined to the scale you intend to use. Most properties can easily be drawn to a scale of either .6 cm to 30 cm (1/4" to 1') or

.3 cm to 30 cm (1/8" to 1'). If you are designing for a small space with many details, select a large scale, such as 2.5 cm to 30 cm (1" to 1')—a good choice for flower bed design. Conversely, a very large lot may require a scale of 2.5 cm to 3 M (1" to 10') in order to fit the entire lot on a single sheet of paper. Remember to leave room for notations about climate, microclimate and soil, which you'll add once the scaled base plan is redrawn.

Some aspects of your base plan can be drawn freehand, but circle and triangle templates are valuable tools for ensuring accuracy. A circle template, for example, will help you indicate the mature spread of particular plants and shrubs, and a triangle will help you draw straight edges.

A soft lead pencil, marked B or F, will be suitable for developing the base plan. Later, a hard lead pencil will be used for detailing the final design. Tracing paper will be necessary for the subsequent development of your designs, allowing you to add details to the scaled base plan on separate sheets.

If you are fortunate, you will have a base plan of your lot from the builder or former owner. Before you breathe a sigh of relief, however, check it to ensure new additions are included. If they aren't you'll have to add them yourself.

Climatic Zones and Microclimates

An essential component of analyzing your site involves studying both the climatic region (or zone) and microclimate of your property. Both will greatly influence your eventual plant selections.

ALBERTA CLIMATE ZONES

LEGEND

1 — 90-110 days Frost Free (-1C)
Ample moisture; low evaporation

2 — 90-110 days Frost Free (-1C)
Precipitation and evaporation varies

2a — 90-100 days Frost Free (-1C)
Precipitation moderate; water table low
Growth often slow

3 — 100-120 days Frost Free (-1C)
Suited to all crops; ideally cool season crops
Moderate moisture; low evaporation

3a — 125-155 days Frost Free (-1C)
Subject to severe chinooks
High evaporation

3b — 120-130 days Frost Free (-1C)
Extremely dry; chinook zone
High evaporation

3c — 100-120 days Frost Free (-1C)
Supplementary water needed
Hot growing season; High evaporation

Data supplied by Alberta Agriculture, Alberta Environment and combined information from the Canadian Department of Agriculture.

When choosing plants, bear in mind that climate zones are guidelines only. For example, a Zone 4 plant might also grow successfully in Zone 2—with a little diligence and extra care.

Climatic zone maps reflect regional climates. They are based on the length of the frost-free period, the average minimum temperature of the coldest month, the average amount of snow cover and the effect of wind in a given region. Being aware of the climatic conditions of your area will help you choose plants that are appropriate for your garden. Check the accompanying zone map to determine your particular growing region.

Though climatic zones vary across the province, generally speaking we have a short season with moderate to low rainfall and severe winter temperatures. But don't be dismayed—thanks to the visionary efforts of Alberta's pioneer plantsmen and today's creative plant breeders, there are more than enough hardy shrubs, trees, vines, perennials and annuals to make delightful gardens. At the end of this chapter, you'll find lists of hardy coniferous and deciduous shrubs and trees suitable for Alberta climatic conditions. Be reminded, however, that you need to learn *all* the cultural requirements of each plant selection before including it in your plan. What will thrive in Cochrane, for example, may not be suitable for Peace River. When in doubt the best solution is to check with your local grower or nursery.

Identifying Your Microclimate

Analyzing the microclimate of your site takes a little more observation and work than measuring plants and structures because each microclimate is unique. But given the benefits of knowing what will thrive best in each area of your garden, the results are well worth the effort. To identify your garden's micro-climate, you take note of the general climate in your neighbourhood and then determine the specifics of your particular site. You may be surprised to find that different parts of your garden will sustain plants not typically suited to the overall climatic zone for your region. Analyze at least the following and record all findings on your scaled base plan:

1. The location of your lot, the size and shape of your house, the number and size of surrounding trees and neighbouring buildings. These factors will influence the climate variances in your garden. Large trees, for example, will draw water from deep in the earth and cool the area surrounding them.

2. The colour of fences and other large structures. Light colours will reflect more light, which makes the surrounding soil warmer and drier.

3. The temperature of particular areas. Thermometers placed in strategic locations can help determine the miniclimates throughout your garden. For example, low-lying areas collect cold denser air and are prone to frost.

4. The amount of sun each area of your garden receives each day.

5. The amount of shade cast by trees and structures. Determine where the biggest shadows fall each day and for how long, remembering that these will change as the season progresses.

6. The prevailing winds and resulting tunnels, if any. North winds bring cooler Arctic air, as do winds blowing off large bodies of nearby water. Take note of when winds typically appear.

7. The areas where water pools after rains.

Analyzing Soil

Soil analysis is the final and perhaps most complex stage in taking stock of your present landscape. Soil zones across the province vary dramatically, as do soil conditions from garden to garden. Soil quality, for example, depends on many factors, including pH, texture, structure and moisture retention. Because soil is a complex ecosystem it is best to invest in a professional soil test. For a small fee, independent laboratories and Alberta Agriculture will provide a comprehensive and accurate quality assessment of your soil.

A site analysis will provide you with a scaled base plan of your site and everything it has to offer.

One factor that you can test for yourself on a seasonal basis is moisture retention. A day or so after a good rainfall, take a handful of soil, squeeze it lightly and open your hand. If the soil stays tightly glued together, it has too much clay and you should add peat moss and compost to increase the soil's porosity. If the soil crumbles quickly, it is too sandy—water and nutrients will drain away too quickly. Add good black loam with a high percentage of organic matter. Somewhere in between, where the soil holds its shape and then crumbles slowly, is close to ideal. Remember to add notes on the condition of your soil to your scaled base plan.

In gathering the information for your base plan, you may have found yourself in corners of your yard that you seldom visit. Sometimes these remote areas offer overlooked potential and hidden treasures. Ask yourself if these could be the sites of new perennial gardens with lots of peonies, delphiniums and garden phlox or places for birdbaths tucked away under tree branches. Many ideas will have come to mind as you've measured and noted the features of your landscape, and that is as it should be—an open mind is the best way to capitalize on the unique qualities that your site has to offer.

STEP THREE: DEVELOPING A BUBBLE PLAN

You have now assembled all the information on the physical features of your property. This base plan, together with the family wish list, will guide you in creating a series of drawings in which you explore different design concepts for your garden.

These *bubble plans,* as they are called, use irregular shapes to roughly map out the general uses you plan to make of different areas in your garden.

Now is a good time to briefly explore the specialty garden chapters following this one to unearth a host of design possibilities for your site. You will discover, for example, how a small front yard slope can be transformed into a colourful rockery, or how a shady unkempt corner can soon feature blooming plants and charming statuary. From water gardens to rose gardens, these specialty garden chapters will help you develop your site's potential. Once you have a good idea of what you'd like, return to Step Three to develop a bubble plan.

With some preliminary ideas in mind, place a clean sheet of tracing paper on top of your base plan, and experiment with a variety of general designs. Try experimenting with rectangles, squares, circles and free-flowing curves to see how the spatial elements of each part of your garden will influence one another. Keep in mind that the basic elements of design—balance, rhythm and proportion—will create a sense of harmony and unity.

Bubble plans represent a quick method of exploring different design area combinations.

Having determined in general the areas that will contain plants and structures, you should now look at their interaction. You may wish to locate a potting shed next to a proposed cutting garden. Or you may want to link two garden areas with an attractive flagstone path. Be mindful that paths should generally take the shortest route through an area since people will tend to take these routes anyway. Remember, as well, how your plan will be viewed from both inside and outside your house. You may, for instance, want to see the children's garden or play area from the kitchen window, or you might decide on a privacy screen next to your patio.

The point is to experiment with different arrangements and combinations of bubble areas, ensuring that they do not conflict with information on your base plan. When you discover an arrangement that pleases you, you are ready for Step Four.

STEP FOUR: DEVELOPING A PLANTING STRATEGY AND CONCEPT DRAWING
Planting Strategies

Developing a planting strategy involves selecting and arranging plants that will be used in the garden composition. It begins with establishing the framework of larger trees (often called *specimen trees*) that anchor your design to the surrounding landscape. From there you select the intermediate and low-growing trees, shrubs and vines that establish the backdrop for border and island flower plantings. The plants you choose should reflect your family's Wish List and be suitable for the growing conditions in your yard. With your garden framework in place, you can turn to the following chapters to guide you in designing specialty gardens for virtually any space or growing conditions that you encounter.

Work your planting strategy out on a plain piece of paper. It will be transferred to an intermediate concept drawing later. Your first concern will be with choosing larger deciduous and coniferous trees. Your choices should offer four-season interest in the garden. Remember that winter interest can be provided by more than just conifers. Dramatic winter settings can be created by the branching patterns, the colour and texture of bark and the colour of berries of a number of deciduous trees. Consider the laurel leaf willow (*Salix pentandra*). Though not a true weeping willow, it has airy descending branches that lead the eye downward. For a beautiful display of winter colour, try the American and European mountain ash (*Sorbus americana* or *Sorbus aucuparia*), which retain their brilliant red berries.

Add a splash of colour to your front garden with mauve-blue Siberian irises and bright yellow pansies. Perfect for dappled shade.

For plants of intermediate height your choices can extend through a wide selection of coniferous and deciduous shrubs. Both the Wichita and Medora junipers (*Juniperus scopulorum* 'Wichita Blue' and *Juniperus scopulorum* 'Medora') and the Brandon and Woodward's globe cedars (*Thuja occidentalis* 'Brandon' and *Thuja occidentalis* 'Woodwardii') offer interesting forms that can be combined with spring flowering shrubs to good effect. The saskatoon (*Amelanchier alnifolia*), northern gold forsythia (*Forsythia ovata* x 'Northern Gold'), Waterton mockorange (*Philadelphus lewisii* 'Waterton') and Nanking cherry (*Prunus tomentosa*) are also excellent choices for Alberta gardens.

Your selection of intermediate-height plants should include the occasional use of accent plants, which add variety to the design. You may wish to use a selection from your "most wanted" species—for example, a colourful shrub rose or a double flowering plum (*Prunus triloba* 'Multiplex') behind a group of low-growing junipers.

Once you've made suitable choices for your framework plantings, consider spacing in arranging the shrubbery plan. It is generally acceptable to have the branches meld together. This slight overlap unifies and strengthens the overall design.

As you plan for the tree and shrub framework of your garden, you should be mindful of the mature height and spread of your selections and of how long they will take to reach mature size. The cutleaf weeping birch, for instance, may look charming in its infancy on a small half-sized lot, but as a full-grown 20-metre (66') tree with an 8-metre (26') spread, it will eliminate views from both inside and outside of the house. If you live in a new neighbourhood and are desperate for greenery while your specimen trees develop, consider faster-growing species to act as short-term fillers.

You should also consider the practical as well as the aesthetic effects of your selections. Trees and large shrubs can frame pleasant views and block unsightly ones. They can also screen visual intrusions from adjoining properties and buffer noises from a busy street.

Garden design, like other art forms, is continually evolving, and an important part of your planting strategy should be to break with some traditions of the past. An excellent place to start is to extend your outdoor living space to the place where we've characteristically least expected it—the front yard. In the past, the front yard provided the necessary curb appeal, unified the house with its surroundings and extended an invitation to guests. Guests were then shuffled off to the backyard—the great outdoor garden room. Traditionally, front yard specimen trees stood alone in the middle of a vast expanse of grass. Provided that they didn't block the entire living room view and that the mature height and width were in proportion to the house, they could be effective in garden design.

But times have changed. Today, the front yard has become an integral part of our outdoor living area as we strive to make more efficient use of shrinking suburban lot sizes. Front lawns are being replaced with spring flowering shrubs, roses, wildflowers and herbaceous borders. Gardeners are taking their special expertise, finely tuned from experience in the backyard, and investing it in the front yard. Interesting garden patios,

Fiery red petunias, brilliant marigolds and a window box of cascading lobelia and geraniums extend a warm welcome.

An enchantingly untidy array of calendulas, poppies, bachelor buttons and flax adds informal charm to the front garden.

paths and creative combinations of plant material now ensure that first impressions are lasting ones. Before you turn to the traditional ideas of a single specimen tree, a few shrubs at the base of the house and a well-manicured expanse of lawn, consider a framework that sets the stage for gardens that surprise and delight.

Front Garden Ideas

1. Intricate patterns of low-growing perennials and herbs surrounding garden statuary will please formal style fanciers.

2. A casual more expansive look can be created by adding a vine-clad arbor to frame the front entrance or to welcome visitors with fragrance and colour.

3. Subtle additions of perennial colour will add interest to informal arrangements of shrubs and trees.

4. If your front walkway is just a narrow ribbon of concrete, improve its appearance by adding rectangular paving stones along the edges, installed on their sides in a prepared sand bed.

5. When planning a new front pathway, allow enough space for two people walking side by side. Concrete doesn't have to be boring—you can seed it with pretty stones, colour it or stamp it with patterns.

6. Surfaces of patio pavers in herringbone, basketweave or a running pattern provide interest and strengthen the overall design if chosen to complement existing brick colours.

7. A brick or wooden planter wrapped around the perimeter of a front garden patio and softened with cascading annuals will provide a welcome evening retreat. Remember, rhythm through repetition will serve to unify design elements.

8. Garden structures can be tucked around the side entrance, enticing guests to explore your backyard garden treasures.

The accompanying reference charts at the end of this chapter represent an extensive selection of hardy coniferous and deciduous shrubs and trees suitable for framework plantings in most gardens across Alberta. Other species and cultivars, which may be suited to only certain areas of the province, are not listed. Local nurseries, garden centres and horticulturalists will be able to offer you more selections and specific cultural requirements for materials particularly suited to your area.

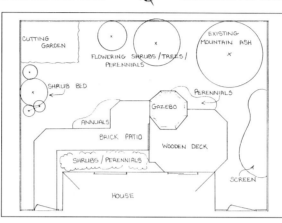

A concept drawing represents your final opportunity to explore and refine design ideas before committing them to a working drawing.

Concept Drawings

With the final choice of bubble plan completed, and your planting strategy and site analysis close at hand, you can move to an intermediate concept drawing. In this stage, you begin refining the exact shapes and dimensions of the planting areas and physical structures. Part of this stage also involves deciding whether you want the naturalistic curved lines of an informal garden or the straight lines and geometric shapes of a formal garden. Another aspect involves beginning to make some decisions about materials for construction. For example, you may decide you want a brick patio, but you don't have to decide yet on the colour and arrangement of bricks. Whatever your choices, remember that your eventual concept drawing should reflect the principles of balance, rhythm and proportion, and colour, texture and form. A large amur maple that blocks the view of a beautiful dwarf blue spruce simply won't do.

Lay a fresh sheet of tracing paper over your base plan, and using your bubble plan and planting strategy as guides, begin to experiment with a variety of styles until you settle on a pleasing composition, remembering that it costs a lot less to change your mind on paper than it does to replant a garden.

STEP FIVE: WORKING DRAWINGS

The final step of the design process is the working drawing, which translates your intermediate concept drawing into a detailed plan by indicating the kind, size and number of plants or structural items that will be included in your garden.

Begin the working drawing by placing another fresh overlay of tracing paper on the base plan and draw to scale all the features of your garden design. For a neater drawing, use a hard lead pencil and apply even pressure while twirling the pencil slowly as you move the lead over the paper. A circle template will help you draw circles to symbolize plant forms. It offers the easiest method of determining the quantity of plants for a given area because all plant material is represented in its mature size. Simply take the square footage of the area and divide this by the space required by each plant. This formula is especially helpful when designing flower beds or areas to be planted with ground-hugging perennials.

The working drawing should be as exact and detailed as possible. The type of fence, the direction of lumber on a deck, the pattern of paving stones and the names of plants are all required, especially if you will need quotations from a landscape contractor. Be sure, as well, to use the different symbols for deciduous and coniferous shrubs and trees on your working drawing. Occasionally, in a very detailed garden design, it may be necessary to identify individual plants with a code. In this case, the letters of the alphabet work well. Whatever code you decide to use, it should be easy to understand and placed in a legend at the top right-hand corner of your plan. This will help keep your plan organized.

At some point during this final step, you should take the working drawing outside to reexamine your plan. Ask yourself again if it meets your family's needs, and if you have chosen hardy plant materials that will provide four seasons of interest. Next, check again to ensure that the mature size of selected plants is appropriate for your site. This double-checking allows you to catch anything you may have overlooked earlier, such as a mature tree blocking too much light from the front window. Now is also the time to confirm that you've selected construction material suited to the architecture of your home. For example, a brick pathway between different garden areas complements a house with brick features. Finally, double-check your site and design for potential additions that will give your garden a personal touch—perhaps a whimsical piece of statuary or a weathered sundial will do the trick. When you are pleased with your working drawing, you can have blueprints made. Make at least two copies, as one inevitably gets forgotten outside in the rain. With Step Five complete, your wish list is about to come true.

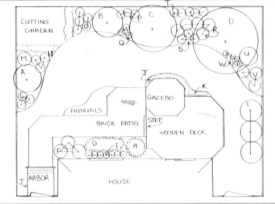

A – Double Flowering Plum	*Prunus triloba* 'Multiplex'
B – Preston Lilac	*Syringa x prestoniae*
C – Ornamental Crabapple	*Malus x* 'Almey'
D – European Mountain Ash	*Sorbus aucuparia*
E – Tower Poplar	*Populus x canescens* 'Tower'
F – Froebel's Spirea	*Spiraea x bumalda* 'Froebelii'
G – Blue Chip Juniper	*Juniperus horizontalis* 'Blue Chip'
H – Dwarf Mugo Pine	*Pinus mugo* var. *pumilo*
I – Siberian Iris	*Iris sibirica*
J – Jackmann's Clematis	*Clematis x jackmannii*
K – Annual Stocks	*Matthiola incana*
L – Daylily	*Hemerocallis* spp.
M – Jens Munk Rose	*Rosa x* 'Jens Munk'
N – Asiatic Lily	*Lilium* spp.
O – Columbine	*Aquilegia* spp.
P – Bee Balm	*Monarda didyma*
Q – Globeflower	*Trollius* spp.
R – Purple Leaved Sandcherry	*Prunus x cistena*
S – Bearded Iris	*Iris x germanica*
T – Delphinium	*Delphinium* spp.
U – Three Lobed Spirea	*Spiraea trilobata*
V – Hybrid Tea Rose	*Rosa x* 'Peace'
W – Carpathian Bellflower	*Campanula carpatica*

The working drawing is the final step of the design process. It contains every detail of your design proposal, including the exact measurements of structures, the patterns and arrangements of construction materials and the locations and numbers of plants. A quickly referenced plant list code will make your design look less cluttered and more professional.

DECIDUOUS TREES

COMMON NAME	BOTANICAL NAME	HEIGHT	SPREAD
Amur Maple	*Acer ginnala*	4–5 M (13–16')	4–5 M (13–16')
Manitoba Maple	*Acer negundo*	14 M (46')	14 M (46')
Ohio Buckeye	*Aesculus glabra*	6–8 M (20–26')	5 M (16')
Red Alder	*Alnus rugosa*	5 M (16')	5–7 M (16–23')
Water Birch	*Betula occidentalis*	6–8 M (20–26')	6–8 M (20–26')
European White Birch	*Betula pendula*	15 M (49')	6 M (20')
Cutleaf Weeping Birch	*Betula pendula* 'Gracilis'	20 M (66')	8 M (26')
Delta Hackberry	*Celtis occidentalis* 'Delta'	10–12 M (33–39')	8 M (26')
Toba Hawthorn	*Crataegus* x *mordenensis* 'Toba'	3–5 M (10–16')	4 M (13')
Russian Olive	*Eleagnus angustifolia*	4–6 M (13–20')	4–6 M (13–20')
Manchurian Ash	*Fraxinus mandschurica*	10 M (33')	8 M (26')
Fallgold Black Ash	*Fraxinus nigra* 'Fallgold'	10 M (33')	3–5 M (10–16')
Patmore Green Ash	*Fraxinus pennsylvanica* var. *subintegerrima* 'Patmore'	2 M (7')	8–10 M (26–33')
Flowering Crabapple	*Malus* spp.	varies	4–5 M (13–16')
Siberian Flowering Crabapple	*Malus baccata*	5 M (16')	5–7 M (16–23')
Almey Rosybloom Crabapple	*Malus* x 'Almey'	3–4 M (10–13')	3–4 M (10–13')
Makamik Crabapple	*Malus* x 'Makamik'	3 M (10')	3 M (10')
Thunderchild Crabapple	*Malus* x 'Thunderchild'	5 M (16')	4 M (13')
Poplar	*Populus* spp.	10–30 M (33–98')	1.5–20 M (5–66')
Amur Cherry	*Prunus maackii*	12 M (39')	10 M (33')
Mayday	*Prunus padus* var. *commutata*	12 M (39')	10–12 M (33–39')
Pincherry	*Prunus pennsylvanica*	5 M (16')	3 M (10')
Schubert Chokecherry	*Prunus virginiana* var. *melanocarpa* 'Schubert'	8 M (26')	8 M (26')
Ussurian Pear	*Pyrus ussuriensis*	8 M (26')	5 M (16')
Bur Oak	*Quercus macrocarpa*	12–15 M (39–49')	10–12 M (33–39')
Siberian White Willow	*Salix alba* 'Sericea'	12 M (39')	12 M (39')
Golden Willow	*Salix alba* 'Vitellina'	15 M (49')	15 M (49')
Laurel Leaf Willow	*Salix pentandra*	12–15 M (39–49')	12–15 M (39–49')
American Mountain Ash	*Sorbus americana*	4–6 M (13–20')	5 M (16')
European Mountain Ash	*Sorbus aucuparia*	4–6 M (13–20')	5 M (16')
Western Mountain Ash	*Sorbus scopulina*	5 M (16')	3 M (10')
Japanese Tree Lilac	*Syringa reticulata*	5 M (16')	3–5 M (10–16')
Morden Littleleaf Linden	*Tilia cordata* 'Morden'	10–12 M (33–39')	5 M (16')
Dropmore Linden	*Tilia* x *flavescens* 'Dropmore'	10–12 M (33–39')	6 M (20')
Brandon Elm	*Ulmus americana* 'Brandon'	30 M (98')	15 M (49')

FOLIAGE COLOUR	SHAPE	COMMENTS
green	broadly spreading	outstanding fruit and foliage colour
green	broadly spreading	good playground tree, aphid prone
green	upright oval	needs shelter, good specimen, unusual blooms and fruit
green	upright spreading	good for moist areas and naturalizing
green	globular	shining reddish brown bark doesn't peel
green	upright oval	white bark, attractive as multistem
green	weeping	white bark, finely cut leaves
green	upright oval	edible fruit, worthy of trial
green	upright spreading	compact, showy pink blooms
silver	spreading	fragrant blooms, good contrast
light green	upright oval	good autumn colour
green	pyramidal	extended autumn colour, best in moist sites
green	upright spreading	good autumn colour, no seeds produced
green to purple	broadly spreading	many pastel shades, prolific blooms
green	broadly spreading	showy blooms and fruit, prone to Fireblight
green	upright spreading	deep rosy-red blooms with white base
purple green	upright spreading	light pink blooms
purple green	globular	soft pink blooms, nice contrast with foliage
green	varies	many species and cultivars, use with discretion
green	upright spreading	golden exfoliating bark, prone to low temperature injury
green	upright spreading	good spring colour, prone to insects, fruit drop
green	upright oval	four-season interest, edible fruit
wine red	upright spreading	single or multistemmed, attractive accent
glossy green	upright oval	outstanding spring blooms, good autumn colour, fruit drop
green	upright oval	slow growing, large shade tree
silver	broadly spreading	excellent contrast, best in moist locations
green	broadly spreading	bright golden bark, best in large landscapes
glossy green	broadly spreading	good playground tree, needs space
green	upright spreading	four-season interest, attracts birds
green	globular	four-season interest, attracts birds, prone to winter injury
green	globular	best in moist and sunny locations, good for naturalizing
green	upright spreading	cream-coloured blooms, late flowering, best multistemmed
green	pyramidal	fragrant flowers, excellent autumn colour
green	pyramidal	fragrant flowers, good autumn colour
green	upright spreading	susceptible to Dutch Elm Disease but a worthy landscape tree

DECIDUOUS SHRUBS AND VINES

COMMON NAME	BOTANICAL NAME	HEIGHT	SPREAD
Shrubs			
Saskatoon	*Amelanchier alnifolia*	3 M (10')	2 M (7')
Common Caragana	*Caragana arborescens*	4 M (13')	4 M (13')
Fernleaf Caragana	*Caragana arborescens* 'Lorbergii'	2 M (7')	2 M (7')
Walker Caragana	*Caragana arborescens* 'Walker'	varies	varies
Tartarian Silver-Leaved Dogwood	*Cornus alba* 'Argenteo-marginata'	1 M (3')	2 M (7')
Siberian Coral Dogwood	*Cornus alba* 'Sibirica'	1 M (3')	1 M (3')
Red Osier Dogwood	*Cornus sericea*	2 M (7')	2 M (7')
Gold Twig Dogwood	*Cornus sericea* 'Flaviramea'	2 M (7')	2 M (7')
Cotoneaster Hedge	*Cotoneaster lucidus*	2 M (7')	2 M (7')
Golden Broom	*Cytisus ratisbonensis*	1 M (3')	1 M (3')
Rock Garden Broom	*Cytisus decumbens* 'Vancouver Gold'	50 cm (20")	1 M (3')
Dwarf Narrow Leaved Burning Bush	*Euonymus nana* 'Turkestanica'	60 cm (2')	1 M (3')
Northern Gold Forsythia	*Forsythia ovata* x 'Northern Gold'	1–2 M (3–7')	1–2 M (3–7')
Lydia Woadwaxen	*Genista lydia*	60 cm (2')	1 M (3')
Dyer's Greenwood	*Genista tinctoria* 'Rossica'	60 cm (2')	1 M (3')
Pee Gee Hydrangea	*Hydrangea paniculata* 'Grandiflora'	1 M (3')	1 M (3')
Zabel's Honeysuckle	*Lonicera korolkowii* 'Zabelii'	2 M (7')	2 M (7')
Vienna Honeysuckle	*Lonicera x xylosteoides* 'Clavey's Dwarf'	50 cm–1 M (18–36")	50 cm–1 M (18–36")
Waterton Mockorange	*Philadelphus lewisii* 'Waterton'	1–2 M (3–7')	1–2 M (3–7')
Minnesota Snowflake Mockorange	*Philadelphus x virginalis* 'Minnesota Snowflake'	1–2 M (3–7')	1–2 M (3–7')
Dart's Gold Ninebark	*Physocarpus opulifolius* 'Dart's Gold'	1 M (3')	1 M (3')
Abbotswood Potentilla	*Potentilla fruticosa* 'Abbotswood'	1 M (3')	1 M (3')
Goldfinger Potentilla	*Potentilla fruticosa* 'Goldfinger'	1 M (3')	1 M (3')
Tangerine Potentilla	*Potentilla fruticosa* 'Tangerine'	1 M (3')	1 M (3')
Cherry Prinsepia	*Prinsepia sinensis*	1–2 M (3–7')	1–2 M (3–7')
Double Flowering Plum	*Prunus triloba* 'Multiplex'	2–3 M (7–10')	2–3 M (7–10')
Nanking Cherry	*Prunus tomentosa*	2 M (7')	2 M (7')
Purple Leaved Sandcherry	*Prunus x cistena*	1–1.5 M (3–5')	1 M (3')
Muckle Plum	*Prunus x nigrella* 'Muckle'	4–5 M (13–16')	4 M (13')
Staghorn Sumac	*Rhus typhina*	2–3 M (7–10')	2–3 M (7–10')
Rose	*Rosa* spp. See 'The Rose Garden,' p. 82		
Coyote Willow	*Salix exigua*	4–5 M (13–16')	4–5 M (13–16')
Purple Osier Willow	*Salix purpurea* 'Gracilis'	1 M (3')	1 M (3')
Red Elder	*Sambucus racemosa*	3 M (10')	3 M (10')
Golden Elder	*Sambucus racemosa* 'Plumosa Aurea'	2–3 M (7–10')	2–3 M (7–10')
Russet Buffaloberry	*Shepherdia canadensis*	3 M (10')	2 M (7')
Silver Buffaloberry	*Shepherdia argentea*	3–5 M (10–16')	4 M (13')
Goldmound Spirea	*Spiraea japonica* 'Goldmound'	1 M (3')	1 M (3')
Three-Lobed Spirea	*Spiraea trilobata*	1 M (3')	1 M (3')
Crispa Spirea	*Spiraea x bumalda* 'Crispa'	50 cm (20")	50 cm (20")
Froebelii Spirea	*Spiraea x bumalda* 'Froebelii'	1 M (3')	1 M (3')
Gold Flame Spirea	*Spiraea x bumalda* 'Gold Flame'	1 M (3')	1 M (3')
Bridalwreath Spirea	*Spiraea x vanhouttei*	1–2 M (3–7')	1–2 M (3–7')
Snowberry	*Symphoricarpos albus*	1.5 M (5')	1.5 M (5')

FOLIAGE COLOUR	SHAPE	FLOWERS	COMMENTS
green	upright leggy	white	spring blooms, edible fruit, autumn colour
dull green	upright	yellow	best for windbreaks and hedges, aggressive
green	upright arching	yellow	fine foliage, graceful weeping habit
green	pendulous	yellow	grafted pendulous form
variegated green-white	rounded	white	good for low-light conditions, good bark colour
soft green	upright	white	blue fruit clusters, red bark adds winter interest
green	upright spreading	white	good autumn colour, tolerates moist locations
green	upright spreading	white	golden bark colour, some tip kill
shiny green	upright spreading	pink	various design applications (hedge, topiary, autumn colour)
light green	globular	sulphur yellow	attractive summer blooms
green	low spreading	bright yellow	abundant flowers, good ground cover, needs winter protection
green	upright to globular	green yellow	bright orange capsules in autumn
green	upright spreading	yellow	early spring colour, buds subject to winterkill
light green	mound spreading	golden yellow	outstanding floral display
light green	upright spreading	bright yellow	extended summer blooming
green	upright spreading	pink	good flowering for semi-shade
green	upright spreading	deep rosy pink	prone to aphid attack, outstanding floral display
green	ball shaped	not applicable	dense dwarf plant
green	ball shaped	white	spring blooms, scentless
green	upright leggy	white	star-burst-shaped blooms, fragrant
golden	mound shaped	white	good accent plant
dull green	globular	white	prolific display
dull green	globular	bright yellow	extended flowering season, effective in groupings
dull green	upright spreading	copper yellow	extended flowering season, effective in groupings
green	upright	inconspicuous	thorns, attractive red fruit
green	upright spreading	pale to deep pink	spring colour, can be pruned to a variety of shapes
green	upright spreading	pinkish	spring colour, edible fruit
deep purple	upright	white to pink	attractive foliage, some winterkill
green	upright spreading	pink	prolific spring blooms
green	upright leggy	green	good autumn colour
silver grey	upright spreading	inconspicuous	weeping form, nice colour contrast
blue green	mound	inconspicuous	good for mass plantings
green	upright arching	white	spring flowers and summer berries
dull golden	upright	white	colourful foliage
dull green	ball shaped	inconspicuous	fruit good for attracting wildlife
silver	irregular	inconspicuous	excellent foliage and fruit colour
green	mound	pink	compact, best in mass plantings
green	ball shaped	white	neat growth habit
reddish green	mound	rosy pink	intense pink blooms, best in mass plantings
reddish green	mound	rosy pink	extended summer bloom, good foliage colour
reddish gold	mound	dull pink	compact, best in mass plantings
green	upright arching	white	graceful arching branches
green	upright	white	good for naturalizing

COMMON NAME	BOTANICAL NAME	HEIGHT	SPREAD
Shrubs continued			
Meyer Lilac	*Syringa meyeri*	2 M (7')	2 M (7')
Common Lilac	*Syringa vulgaris* 'Charles Joly'	3 M (10')	3 M (10')
Hyacinth Flowered Lilac	*Syringa* x *hyacinthiflora* 'Sister Justina'	3 M (10')	3 M (10')
Preston Lilac	*Syringa* x *prestoniae* 'Isabella'	3 M (10')	3 M (10')
Wayfaring Tree	*Viburnum lantana*	1.5–2 M (5–7')	1.5–2 M (5–7')
Nannyberry	*Viburnum lentago*	2 M (7')	2 M (7')
American Highbush Cranberry	*Viburnum trilobum*	3 M (10')	2 M (7')
Vines			
Western White Clematis	*Clematis ligusticifolia*	4 M (13')	2 M (7')
Big Petal Clematis	*Clematis macropetala*	2 M (7')	2 M (7')
Ground Clematis	*Clematis recta*	1–1.5 M (3–5')	1–1.5 M (3–5')
Western Blue Clematis	*Clematis verticillaris* var. *columbiana*	3 M (10')	1.5 M (5')
Jackmann's Clematis	*Clematis* x *jackmannii*	4 M (13')	2 M (7')
Dropmore Scarlet Trumpet Honeysuckle	*Lonicera* x *brownii* 'Dropmore Scarlet Trumpet'	2–3 M (7–10')	1 M (3')
Virginia Creeper	*Parthenocissus quinquefolia*	15–20 M (49–66')	5 M (16')
Engelman's Virginia Creeper	*Parthenocissus quinquefolia* 'Engelmannii'	15–20 M (49–66')	5 M (16')

FOLIAGE COLOUR	SHAPE	FLOWERS	COMMENTS
green	ball shaped	rosy purple	compact, very fragrant
green	upright spreading	reddish purple	very fragrant double blooms, tolerates difficult locations
green	upright spreading	white	tall fragrant double blooms
green	ball shaped	rosy pink	late blooming, easy culture
grey green	ball shaped	white	four-season interest
glossy green	upright leggy	white	four-season interest
green	upright spreading	white	four-season interest
green	climber	white	prolific white blooms
green	climber	violet	vigorous climber
green	climber	white	fragrant climber, attractive in white or evening gardens
green	climber	blue	worthy of trial
green	climber	deep purple	prolific blooms
green	climber	orange	good contrast, attracts hummingbirds
green	climber	inconspicuous	vigorous climber, requires support, good autumn colour
green	climber	inconspicuous	vigorous climber, self-attaching, spectacular autumn colour

CONIFEROUS SHRUBS AND TREES

COMMON NAME	BOTANICAL NAME	HEIGHT	SPREAD
Shrubs			
Horizontal Juniper	*Juniperus horizontalis*	60 cm–1 M (2–3')	varies
Blue Chip Juniper	*Juniperus horizontalis* 'Blue Chip'	15 25 cm (6–10")	1 M (3')
Prince of Wales Juniper	*Juniperus horizontalis* 'Prince of Wales'	15–25 cm (6–10")	2–3 M (7–10')
Savin Juniper	*Juniperus sabina*	1 M (3')	2 M (7')
Arcadia Juniper	*Juniperus sabina* 'Arcadia'	60–90 cm (2–3')	2 M (7')
Calgary Carpet Juniper	*Juniperus sabina* 'Calgary Carpet'	1 M (3')	2 M (7')
Rocky Mountain Juniper	*Juniperus scopulorum*	4–5 M (13–16')	1.5–2 M (5–7')
Medora Juniper	*Juniperus scopulorum* 'Medora'	3 M (10')	1.5–2 M (5–7')
Wichita Blue Juniper	*Juniperus scopulorum* 'Wichita Blue'	3 M (10')	1.5–2 M (5–7')
Golden Pfitzer Juniper	*Juniperus* x *media* 'Pfitzerana Aurea'	60 cm (2')	2 M (7')
Nest Spruce	*Picea abies* 'Nidiformis'	1 M (3')	1.5 M (5')
Dwarf Alberta Spruce	*Picea glauca* 'Albertiana Conica'	1–2 M (3–7')	1 M (3')
Dwarf Colorado Blue Spruce	*Picea pungens* 'Glauca globosa'	1–2 M (3–7')	1–2 M (3–7')
Creeping Colorado Blue Spruce	*Picea pungens* 'Glauca procumbens'	50 cm (20")	varies
Bristlecone Pine	*Pinus aristata*	4 M (13')	1.5–3 M (5–10')
Dwarf Mugo Pine	*Pinus mugo* 'Compacta'	1 M (3')	1 M (3')
Dwarf Mugo Pine	*Pinus mugo* 'Teeny'	30–60 cm (1–2')	30–60 cm (1–2')
Dwarf Mugo Pine	*Pinus mugo* var. *pumilo*	50 cm (20")	5 M (16')
White Cedar	*Thuja occidentalis*	8 M (26')	2 M (7')
Brandon Cedar	*Thuja occidentalis* 'Brandon'	2–6 M (7–20')	1.5 M (5')
Woodward's Globe Cedar	*Thuja occidentalis* 'Woodwardii'	1–2 M (3–7')	1.5 M (5')
Trees			
Tamarack	*Larix laricina*	15 M (49')	5 M (16')
Siberian Larch	*Larix sibirica*	15 M (49')	5 M (16')
Norway Spruce	*Picea abies*	15 M (49')	5 M (16')
White Spruce	*Picea glauca*	20 M (66')	5 M (16')
Colorado Spruce	*Picea pungens*	20 M (66')	5 M (16')
Swiss Stone Pine	*Pinus cembra*	12 M (39')	3–5 M (10–16')
Lodgepole Pine	*Pinus contorta* var. *latifolia*	20 M (66')	3–5 M (10–16')
Mugo Pine	*Pinus mugo*	varies	varies
Ponderosa Pine	*Pinus ponderosa*	15 M (49')	5 M (16')
Scots Pine	*Pinus sylvestris*	15 M (49')	5 M (16')
Douglas Fir	*Pseudotsuga menziesii* var. *glauca*	20 M (66')	5 M (16')

COLOUR	FORM	COMMENTS
varies	low spreading	winter interest
blue	low spreading	four-season colour
blue green	low spreading	purplish winter colour
dark green	vase shaped	parent to superior cultivars
bright green	vase shaped	graceful arching branches
bright green	low spreading	good ground cover
varies	pyramidal	parent to superior cultivars
grey blue	compact pyramid	resistant to winter burn
silvery blue	pyramidal	requires shearing
green with yellow tips	upright spreading	prone to winterburn, use with discretion
dark green	nest shaped	unique landscape element
dark green	upright pyramid	susceptible to winter burn
blue	dense globular	good blue colour
blue	prostrate	good in rockeries
dark green	twisted irregular	good in rockeries
green	globular	good in rockeries
dark green	mound shaped	neat growth habit
dark green	upright globular	good in rockeries
green	varies	winter interest
deep green	columnar	vertical design element
light green	globular	globular design element
soft green	pyramidal	excellent autumn colour, autumn needle drop
soft green	pyramidal	adapts to dry-land locations, autumn needle drop
dark green	broad pyramid	pendulous branches
dark green	pyramidal	effective in groupings or as individual specimen
varies	pyramidal	popular specimen tree, many cultivars
dark green	columnar	attractive specimen tree
yellow green	narrow pyramidal	provincial tree, good for naturalizing
dark green	varies	parent of superior cultivars, good for naturalizing
dull green	cylindrical	drought resistant
blue green	pyramidal	form opens with maturity, attractive orange bark
deep green	pyramidal	large specimen tree

THE SPRING GARDEN

"A treasure of well-set jewels"

–Gertrude Jekyll

Spring has always been symbolic of new beginnings. Officially, it arrives March 21, but for winter-weary gardeners, it arrives when the air smells of moist earth and handfuls of prairie crocuses come home with the kids. A spring garden can be an acre of prairie grassland painted blue with the familiar anenome, a dozen tulips tucked in a corner beside the front door or a single bleeding heart with white and pink blooms hanging like coloured charms on a bracelet. With delicate fragrances and myriad shapes and colours, the flowers of spring are the floral hors d'oeuvres of beautiful gardens.

Primroses, known as the flowers of imagination, offer delicate clusters of spring colour. These "first roses" are ideal for naturalizing in moist shady locations.

In *Colour Schemes for the Flower Garden*, British gardening legend Gertrude Jekyll describes her spring garden as the first in "a series of soul-satisfying pictures—a treasure of well-set jewels." An entire garden area was devoted exclusively to spring blooming flowers of "tender colouring—pale Primroses, Daffodils, pale yellow early Iris . . . with drifts of white and pale yellow Tulips."

When autumn garden catalogues display coloured pictures of flowering tulips the size of brandy snifters, the temptation is strong to devote an entire garden area to spring planting. But a wise gardener, at least one without a team of labourers, creates a spring garden within an existing garden to extend seasonal interest and colour. Depending on your site, there are many early flowering perennials, shrubs and trees to choose from.

The first step in creating a spring garden is to decide on its character. Is it to be sunny and cheerful? Subdued and nostalgic? Bold and impressive?

Yellow irises, pink tulips and mauve allium can provide a casual backdrop for low-growing primroses, violas and snow-in-summer. This impressive display gives the garden a sunny and cheerful character.

Select only plants and colours that will contribute to the mood you desire. For example, a thick straight row of elegant red, yellow and white tulips looks impressive alongside a brick sidewalk but perhaps a little overbearing in a small rock garden.

The second step is to consider the views from the kitchen or dining room window and locate your spring display accordingly. Nothing is quite as satisfying as the sight of brilliant spring blooms before evenings can be spent out of doors.

With these ideas in mind, let's look at some ways to create a spring display within your existing garden. From tiny splashes of colour in the rock garden to showy tulips and stately irises in the perennial border to tree branches heavy with delicate blooms, you can incorporate spring features into a wide variety of settings.

EARLY BLOOMS FOR THE ROCK GARDEN

The tapestry of contrasting textures, colours and forms that characterizes the rockery can be as pleasing in spring as later in the growing season if spring flowers are incorporated into your plan. The tiny jewel-like blooms of early spring iris (*Iris reticulata*) are the harbingers of spring in my rock garden. Soon to follow are the creeping phlox (*Phlox subulata*), cascading colour over the rocks with brilliant mats of magenta and lavender. This versatile perennial is also pleasing at the edges of borders and in informal woodland gardens. The summer perennials, such as bellflower (*Campanula* spp.) and summer flowering phlox (*Phlox* spp.), will make their entrance as these spring blooms exit.

If you prefer you can turn the spring rockery into a carpet of grape hyacinths. These minihyacinths offer slender flower stems in blue, pink and white. Grape hyacinths naturalize easily in rock gardens and are also well suited as edging in flower beds and under shrubs and trees. Two species—*Muscari botryoides* and *Muscari armeniacum*—are excellent choices for Alberta rock gardens. Plant them with the delicate nodding blue flowers of Siberian squills (*Scilla sibirica*), also known as bluebells. A cluster of the yellow companion fritillaria (*Fritillaria pallidiflora*) is also showy in the rockery. Bedding-out plants, forget-me-nots (*Myosotis sylvatica*) and viola (*Viola* spp.) can fill in the pockets of colour as these spring flowers fade.

If you enjoy cheerful colours, consider yellow tulips. The species *Tulipa tarda* produces bright yellow and white starry flowers prolifically. Annual nasturtiums (*Nasturtium tropaeolum*) and petunias (*Petunia* x *hybrida*) can follow the tulips to hide their unsightly withered foliage, which must be left to replenish the bulbs for the following year.

Besides colour, scent is also a welcome spring addition to the rock garden. Tucked between protruding pieces of boulders, the tiny white or pink hugging flowers of rockcress (*Arabis alpina*) will provide masses of early spring colour. With its sweet fragrance, this versatile perennial will also delight you beside a patio or edging a garden path. The foliage of rockcress remains throughout the growing season and will provide excellent textural contrast with summer flowering rockery plants.

Other early flowering perennials for the rock

Create a perennial spring tapestry with drifts of purple and white crocuses. Ideal for naturalizing in areas with good snow coverage.

garden include purple rockcress (*Aubrieta deltoidea*) and basket-of-gold (*Aurinia saxatilis*), aptly named for its clumps of yellow rosette flowers. Another favourite is sea pinks (*Armeria maritima*), also known as thrift, which forms tight carpets of blue grasslike foliage bearing chivelike pink, rose and white blossoms.

EARLY BLOOMS FOR THE PERENNIAL GARDEN

In perennial gardens, tulips inaugurate the spring season with their cheerful blooms. They bring endless varieties of flower shapes, from the starry *Tulipa tarda* and *Tulipa turkestanica* to the gentle ruffles of multiflowered varieties. And who can resist enticing cultivar names like 'Burgundy Lace,' 'Fringed Rhapsody' and 'Lilac Perfection'?

For Alberta gardeners, the vast assortment of tulips can make selection mind-boggling. However, a classification system exists that sorts tulips according to time of bloom, parentage and flower form. For early flowering blooms, look for single early or double early cultivars. For midseason colour, choose from the Triumph and Darwin hybrids. Among the late-blooming tulips, select from the pointed arching petals of the lily-flowered varieties or the single late tulips. Parrot and Rembrandt tulips will also extend flowering time in the spring garden. A wise gardener chooses a mixture of early, midseason and late-blooming cultivars.

Besides offering a variety of bloom times, tulips are available in a variety of heights. If you are adding them to an existing garden, be sure to plant the tall varieties at the back and the shorter ones in front. For island tulip beds that are viewed from all sides, plant the tall varieties in the centre. The shorter varieties are then planted in decreasing heights around them.

Tulip colours can be used to evoke the appropriate mood in different parts of your spring perennial garden. Bright cheerful colours, such as the buttercup-yellow blooms of the cultivars 'Hamilton' and 'Jewel of Spring,' add sparkle and extend a warm welcome to the front or door-yard garden. 'Fancy Frills'—a delightful ivory-coloured cultivar with rosy-pink stripes—on stage with 'Pink Fantasy,' the gracious pink lady of parrot tulips, evokes a nostalgic mood. Just as in rockeries, you can mingle early spring irises, squills and grape hyacinths with your tulip selections and enjoy a parade of colour throughout the season.

If your perennial garden tastes run to the tranquil all-white garden, consider incorporating the pure white blooms of the cultivar 'Diana' or the gorgeous, fully double white flowers of 'Mount Tacoma.' These tulips are ideally planted in a sunny location and complemented by early flowering perennial candytuft (*Iberis sempervirens*) as a low-growing companion.

The key to creating a pleasing colour palette throughout the growing season is choosing colours that complement your house. For example, warm yellows and reds look great beside a white, brown or cedar house. Tulips in shades of pink, from soft pastel to vibrant magenta, complement a grey or blue house. Remember, however, that

Tulips inaugurate spring with their satiny blooms. Choose a mixture of early, mid- and late-blooming cultivars in a variety of colours and heights.

these are just guidelines. If you prefer a kaleidoscope of tulip colours, select a mixture of hot pinks and vibrant yellows, whites, oranges and reds. In varying heights, these festival-like colours will create a stunning display.

The annual ritual of planting spring flowering tulip bulbs commences in the autumn. They should be planted as soon in early autumn as they become available to allow them to establish good root systems prior to ground freezing. If an organic mulch of peat moss or well-rotted grass clippings is applied immediately after planting, freezing is delayed slightly, allowing more time for root development and providing protection from temperature extremes.

When selecting a site for your tulip bed, keep in mind that tulips prefer a sunny location. Plant them in well-drained organically enriched soil. The depth of planting depends on the kind and size of bulb as well as the soil type. Generally, tulips are planted 15–20 cm (6–8") deep in loamy soil and 2.5–5 cm (1–2") deeper in sandy soil. The addition of a fertilizer containing a higher ratio of phosphorous is recommended for encouraging root development.

The colourful flags of bearded irises (*Iris* x *germanica*) will with careful planning bloom throughout the spring. Named for the Greek goddess of the rainbow, their multicoloured flowers are considered the aristocrats of early blooming perennials.

The modern bearded iris has a very diverse parentage. These complex hybrids are available in a tremendous range of colours. From the palest lavender, through pinks, rose and peach to crisply fluted white blooms, there's an iris to meet the demands of every garden palette.

Bearded iris flowers consist of three upright petals, called *standards*, and three down-facing petal-like sepals, called *falls*. The *beard* is the fuzzy growth of hairs located on the falls. In iris catalogues, the flowers are often described by their standards and falls.

If you enjoy bearded irises and you wish to expand your collection, consider creating an iris dell in your garden. A dell, of course, refers to contours or gentle rolls in the existing topography. In flat terrain, the contoured effect of the dell is achieved by the laborious method of wheelbarrow-mania. But for your efforts you will be rewarded with rolling drifts of attractive colour. If your neighbour borrowed your wheelbarrow and didn't return it, you can still create the illusion of the dell through grouping irises of varying heights and colours in successive waves.

Bearded irises need full sun for at least half the day and well-drained, deep rich soil to encourage prolific blooming. Although some species thrive in moist conditions, the majority are subject to rot unless excellent drainage is provided.

Columbine, with its curiously spurred flowers, prefers full sun or partial shade and well-drained organically rich soil.

In spring, globeflowers offer buttercuplike flowers in yellow and orange. Blossoms are borne on long stems above attractive dark-green and deeply lobed foliage.

Preparing a New Iris Bed

1. The best time to plant and divide bearded iris is after flowering, in late July or early August. Plan to space the rhizomes 25–30 cm (10–12") apart in groups of three and five for a strong display of colour in a smaller garden, and in groups of five, seven and nine for larger gardens.

2. When preparing a new iris bed, it is good practice to spade in a generous application of compost below the root level.

3. Dig a hole 15–25 cm (6–10") deep.

4. Make an inverted V by mounding the soil, and place the rhizome on top of the V, just below the soil level. Spread the roots carefully on either side.

5. Fill the hole with enriched soil, gently tamping it around the rhizome but leaving the top exposed—it can use all the sun that our short summers provide. Avoid deep planting, which may retard flowering. (Note that in areas where winter losses occur, a covering of soil over the rhizome may be necessary. Also, if your soil is sandy, plant the rhizome at the soil level.)

6. Water your new iris bed well. A low nitrogen fertilizer may be applied as a top dressing around the plants in early spring.

Another favourite early blooming perennial is columbine (*Aquilegia* spp.) with its curiously spurred flowers in soft colours, including white, yellow, red, pink, purple and blue.

Columbines prefer well-drained organically rich soil in a full sun or partial shade location. When planted in front of taller irises, their delicate nodding flowers will hide withered foliage and provide early colour and contrast in the perennial garden.

Bergenias (*Bergenia cordifolia*) are very adaptable early flowering perennials. Their pink flowers and dense cabbagelike leaves make an attractive statement at the front of the perennial border or in a group tucked among evergreen shrubs.

EARLY FLOWERING SHRUBS AND TREES

From the clear white blooms of the Waterton mockorange to the delicate yellow flowers of forsythia to the lavender blooms of the lilac, a broad range of hardy spring flowering shrubs and trees can become an integral part of every Alberta garden's colour palette.

Blossom and foliage colour are primary reasons for including flowering shrubs and trees in spring gardens. The purple leaved sandcherry (*Prunus* x *cistena*) is a favourite for its wine-purple foliage and delicate pink-white blossoms. Even though tip killing sometimes occurs, its contribution to colour in the spring garden is worth the risk. Because it is often grafted on green-leaved rootstock, deeper planting is recommended to discourage suckering. The blooms

The clear white blooms of the mockorange provide a dazzling late spring display. Plant in a sheltered location away from harsh winter winds.

of the double flowering plum (*Prunus triloba* 'Multiplex') can be enjoyed for their scent as well as appearance. Place them near a garden gate, where their delicate fragrance will greet visitors.

Extending seasonal interest is another element to consider in your choice of early flowering shrubs and trees. Be sure to include plant material from the genus *Prunus,* which includes cherries and plums. Attractive hedges that frame colourful perennial borders or conceal unsightly views can be created with a row of Nanking cherry (*Prunus tomentosa*). Their soft pink flowers in spring are followed by small bright red cherries suitable for preserves. Even shadier locations in the garden can enjoy spring blossoms if they contain a cranberry (*Viburnum* spp.), which celebrates spring with a profusion of white blooms. Later in the season, it offers edible fruits and berries, which are often ideal for attracting wildlife well into the autumn.

Few things are as pleasurable as the sweet scent of lilac or the sight of the rosy blooms on an ornamental flowering crabapple. Paramount to including shrubs and trees in your spring garden plan is placing them where your senses can best appreciate them. They should be among the first sights and fragrances to greet your return to the garden in spring.

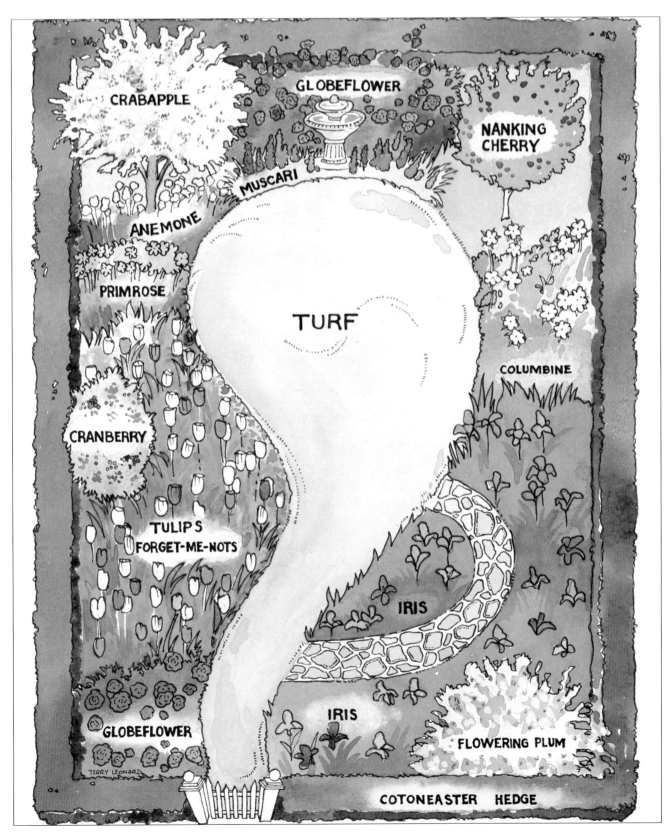

This spring garden draws on pastel colours, scented perennials and profusely blooming shrubs and trees to create a bold effect within a natural informal design.

THE SPRING GARDEN

COMMON NAME	BOTANICAL NAME	HEIGHT	SPREAD
Perennials			
Carpet Bugleweed	*Ajuga reptans*	10 cm (4")	30 – 45 cm (12–18")
Prairie Crocus	*Anemone patens*	10 – 25 cm (4–10")	varies
Snowdrop Anemone	*Anemone sylvestris*	30 – 45 cm (12–18")	30 – 45 cm (12–18")
Columbine	*Aquilegia* spp.	30 – 60 cm (12–24")	30 – 60 cm (12–24")
Rockcress	*Arabis alpina*	15 – 20 cm (6–10")	30 – 40 cm (12–16")
Sea Pink	*Armeria maritima*	10 – 30 cm (4–12")	10 – 30 cm (4–12")
Alpine Aster	*Aster alpinus*	20 – 25 cm (8–10")	20 – 30 cm (8–12")
Purple Rockcress	*Aubrieta deltoidea*	15 cm (6")	varies
Basket-of-Gold	*Aurinia saxatilis*	25 – 30 cm (10–12")	varies
Bergenia	*Bergenia cordifolia*	30 – 45 cm (12–18")	varies
Snow-in-Summer	*Cerastium tomentosum*	15 – 30 cm (6–12")	varies
Lily-of-the-Valley	*Convallaria majalis*	10 – 20 cm (4–8")	varies
Bleeding Heart	*Dicentra spectablis*	90 cm (36")	90 cm (36")
White Bleeding Heart	*Dicentra spectablis* 'Alba'	60 cm (24")	60 cm (24")
Shooting Star	*Dodecatheon meadia*	30 cm (12")	15 cm (6")
Draba	*Draba aizoides*	10 cm (4")	15 cm (6")
Cushion Spurge	*Euphorbia epithymoides*	30 – 45 cm (12–18")	45 – 55 cm (18–22")
Cranesbill Geranium	*Geranium sanguineum*	30 – 40 cm (12–16")	30 – 40 cm (12–16")
Perennial Candytuft	*Iberis sempervirens*	30 cm (12")	30 – 50 cm (12–20")
Forget-Me-Not	*Myosotis sylvatica*	30 cm (12")	30 – 40 cm (12–16")
Creeping Phlox	*Phlox subulata*	10 – 15 cm (4–6")	10 – 20 cm (4–8")
Primrose	*Primula* spp.	varies	varies
Ewer's Stonecrop	*Sedum ewersii*	30 cm (12")	30 cm (12")
Globeflower	*Trollius* spp.	40 – 90 cm (16–36")	25 – 90 cm (10–36")
Periwinkle	*Vinca minor*	10 – 15 cm (4–6")	30 – 45 cm (12–18")
Bulbs and Others			
Blue Globe Onion	*Allium caeruleum*	60 cm (24")	varies
Ostrowsky Onion	*Allium ostrowskianum*	15 cm (6")	varies
Glory-of-the-Snow	*Chionodoxa lucilliae*	15 – 25 cm (6–10")	varies
Crocus	*Crocus* spp.	10 – 15 cm (4–6")	varies
Fritillaria	*Fritillaria pallidiflora*	30 – 45 cm (12–18")	varies
Danfordiae Iris	*Iris danfordiae*	10 – 15 cm (4–6")	varies
Early Spring Iris	*Iris reticulata*	10 – 15 cm (4–6")	varies
Bearded Iris	*Iris x germanica*	varies	varies
Grape Hyacinth	*Muscari armeniacum*	20 – 23 cm (8–9")	varies
Grape Hyacinth	*Muscari botryoides*	15 – 25 cm (6–10")	varies
Daffodil	*Narcissus* spp.	15 – 45 cm (6–18")	varies
Squill	*Scilla* spp.	10 – 15 cm (4–6")	varies
Siberian Squill	*Scilla sibirica*	10 – 15 cm (4–6")	varies

FOLIAGE COLOUR	FLOWER COLOUR	COMMENTS
purple green	blue	showy en masse, good ground cover
green	bluish purple	delicate flowers, good for naturalizing
green	white	good for underplantings but can be invasive
green	wide variety	best in partial shade
grey	pink to white	fragrant, good in rockeries
green	magenta pink	fragrant blooms, interesting grasslike foliage
dull green	blue to white	extended blooming, good in rockeries
green	purple	mat forming, good in rockeries
grey green	yellow	ideal in rockeries
glossy green	rosy pink	evergreen, bronzes in autumn
silver	white	rampant spreading, good colour contrast
green	white	fragrant blooms
green	pink with white	arching branches with pink heart-shaped blooms
green	white	excellent for white gardens
green	bright pink	unique flower, good in rockeries
green	yellow	good in rockeries and alpine gardens
green	yellow	tolerates heat and drought, soft spring colour
green	purple to magenta	attractive foliage, good in rockeries
green	white	fragrant blooms, underplant with tulips, good in rockeries
green	blue	delicate blooms
green	red, pink, purple, white	showy blooms, matlike ground cover
green	wide variety	showy en masse, good in rockeries
blue	pink	unusual flower, drought tolerant ground cover
green	yellow and orange	showy blooms, lovely cut flower, good for naturalizing
green	blue	trailing habit, ground cover, use for underplanting
green	blue	attractive globe-shaped blooms
green	pink	attractive pink blooms
green	pink, blue, white	early delicate spring blooms
green	wide variety	delightful spring colour, good for naturalizing
green	yellow	striking blooms, good accent
green	yellow	perfect in rockeries
green	wide variety	fragrant carpet of bloom
green	wide variety	rainbow of colours
green	blue	forms thick carpet of colour
green	pink, blue, white	forms thick carpet of colour
green	pink, orange, yellow, cream, white	brilliant colours
green	blue, white	good for naturalizing
green	blue, white	delicate nodding flowers

COMMON NAME	BOTANICAL NAME	HEIGHT	SPREAD
Bulbs and Others continued			
Tulip	*Tulipa* spp.	5–60 cm (2–24")	varies
Tulip	*Tulipa tarda*	5–10 cm (2–4")	varies
Tulip	*Tulipa turkestanica*	10–15 cm (4–6")	varies
Tulip	*Tulipa* 'Burgundy Lace'	70 cm (28")	varies
Tulip	*Tulipa* 'Diana'	35 cm (14")	varies
Tulip	*Tulipa* 'Fancy Frills'	60 cm (24")	varies
Tulip	*Tulipa* 'Fringed Rhapsody'	60 cm (24")	varies
Tulip	*Tulipa* 'Hamilton'	45 cm (18")	varies
Tulip	*Tulipa* 'Jewel of Spring'	60 cm (24")	varies
Tulip	*Tulipa* 'Lilac Perfection'	45 cm (18")	varies
Tulip	*Tulipa* 'Mount Tacoma'	45 cm (18")	varies
Flowering Trees and Shrubs			
Saskatoon	*Amelanchier alnifolia*	3 M (10')	2 M (7')
Toba Hawthorn	*Crataegus* x *mordenensis* 'Toba'	3–5 M (10–16')	4 M (13')
Daphne	*Daphne* spp.	30–60 cm (1–2')	30–60 cm (1–2')
Northern Gold Forsythia	*Forsythia ovata* x 'Northern Gold'	1–2 M (3–7')	1–2 M (3–7')
Flowering Crabapple	*Malus* spp.	varies	4–5 M (13–16')
Waterton Mockorange	*Philadelphus lewisii* 'Waterton'	1–2 M (3–7')	1–2 M (3–7')
Mayday	*Prunus padus* var. *commutata*	12 M (39')	10–12 M (33–39')
Pincherry	*Prunus pennsylvanica*	5 M (16')	2 M (7')
Nanking Cherry	*Prunus tomentosa*	2 M (7')	2 M (7')
Double Flowering Plum	*Prunus triloba* 'Multiplex'	2–3 M (7–10')	2–3 M (7–10')
Purple Leaved Sandcherry	*Prunus* x *cistena*	1–1.5 M (3–5')	1 M (3')
Muckle Plum	*Prunus* x *nigrella* 'Muckle'	4–5 M (13–16')	3–4 M (10–13')
Meyer Lilac	*Syringa meyeri*	2 M (7')	2 M (7')
Common Lilac	*Syringa vulgaris* 'Charles Joly'	3 M (10')	3 M (10')
Hyacinth Flowered Lilac	*Syringa* x *hyacinthiflora* 'Sister Justina'	3 M (10')	3 M (10')
Preston Lilac	*Syringa* x *prestoniae* 'Isabella'	3 M (10')	3 M (10')
Wayfaring Tree	*Viburnum lantana*	1.5–2 M (5–7')	1.5–2 M (5–7')
Nannyberry	*Viburnum lentago*	3 M (10')	2 M (7')
American Highbush Cranberry	*Viburnum trilobum*	2 M (7')	2 M (7')

FOLIAGE COLOUR	FLOWER COLOUR	COMMENTS
green	wide variety	showy blooms
green	yellow and white	ideal in rockeries
green	yellow and white	ideal in rockeries
green	burgundy	good in backs of borders
green	white	attractive en masse
green	pink	blooms have fringed edges
green	yellow	blooms flushed with red, each bloom unique
green	yellow	blooms have fringed edges
green	yellow	good in backs of borders
green	lilac	double blooms, attractive en masse
green	white	fully ruffled blooms
green	white	early blooming
green	pink	showy blooms, good for small gardens
green	pink	fragrant blooms, needs winter protection
green	yellow	very early blooms borne on naked stems
green to purple	green varies	many pastel shades, prolific blooms
green	white	attractive blooms
green	white	attractive spring display
green	white	attractive spring display
green	pale pink	attractive spring display
green	pink	spectacular spring display
deep purple	whitish pink	good contrast
green	bright pink	spectacular spring display
green	rosy purple	showy blooms
green	reddish purple	fragrant and showy
green	white	attractive and fragrant
green	rosy pink	fragrant and showy
silver grey	white	attractive spring display
green	white	attractive spring display
green	white	attractive spring display

THE CHILDREN'S GARDEN

"Know what it is to be child? . . .

it is to turn pumpkins into coaches,

and mice into horses"

–Percy Bysshe Shelley

Many of us who love to garden owe our passion for working with nature to our childhoods. One of my earliest and most poignant garden memories is of gathering bunches of sweetly scented lilacs from the hedge behind our house. I also remember my grandmother showing me how to open snapdragons' jaws and press pansies. Then there were afternoons spent pulling petals off daisies while chanting, "He loves me, he loves me not." And on sultry summer days, we'd link miles of daisies to make necklaces.

The first step to instilling in children a sense of wonder at the variety and splendour of nature is simply letting them explore the garden world. So take your youngsters by the hand and visit the garden. Observe and listen to what they find most interesting. Let them feel the difference between a handful of sand and a handful of organically rich soil. Let them smell the roses and feel their satiny petals or look at the prickles and how they cover the entire stem. Compare the fragrance of roses with the pungent aroma of marigolds. Better still, take a few minutes to help your children construct a daisy chain or clover crown.

Don't worry too much that youngsters will run amok in the garden. With your assistance they will learn quickly what shouldn't be touched, especially if they have their own patch of bright zinnias or nasturtiums to pick when the whim strikes.

Extend your children's activities to learning the names of plants, something for which preschoolers have an insatiable appetite. While exploring the garden, have them point out specific coloured flowers—a yellow one, a red one and so on. Or choose

Children will have fun squeezing open the "jaws" of snapdragons. These sun-loving annuals are available in varying heights and a rainbow of colours.

WARNING: Adults and caregivers are advised that many plants are harmful or poisonous. Children must be made aware of the dangers of tasting any plants, seeds, berries or mushrooms indiscriminately. The sweet pea seeds mentioned in this chapter are poisonous if ingested, so planting must be carefully supervised by adults. For more information about harmful or poisonous substances in the garden consult your local Alberta Agriculture office.

specific characteristics—like satiny petals or prickly flowers. When they find the colour or characteristic, you supply the plant's name. Keeping the activity within the context of a game makes your time together fun, and your children will be discovering the basics of science and nature at the same time.

DESIGNING CHILDREN'S GARDENS

The key elements in designing children's gardens are simple and few. Most important is that children determine the design on their own terms, based on their likes and dislikes. What governs the aesthetics of garden design for adults in terms of balance, rhythm and proportion, and colour, texture and form, doesn't necessarily apply to children's sense of beauty. They may create odd combinations such as a half row of calendula wandering aimlessly into lettuce and a few nasturtiums, but don't worry. Just try to guide the process enough to ensure success. Wherever possible, encourage children to select plants that provide experiences appealing to sight, touch, taste, and smell.

A CHILDREN'S SENSORY GARDEN
Plants to See

For children, waiting for a seed to sprout its first leaves is the hardest part of gardening, so help them choose seeds that sprout quickly. Large pea-sized nasturtium seeds (*Tropaeolum majus*) are easy and fun for small hands to plant, and in a matter of days your children will be rewarded with easy-to-spot round leaves. Annual sweet peas (*Lathyrus odoratus*) and calendula (*Calendula officinalis*) also grow

Children will enjoy the bright colours of annual zinnias. These easy-care plants make perfect indoor bouquets for mom or dad.

quickly from seed and are good choices for young gardeners.

Once their planted seeds have germinated, your children can explore the differences between the young seedlings. Some will be light green while others will be dark. Some will be round leaved and others will be pointed. As the plants mature, the differences between them will become more visible, and children can turn their curiosity to vibrant colours and interesting flower forms. Bold colours—reds, yellows and oranges—impart feelings of warmth and are cheerful for children to look at. Nasturtium petals, the colours of pumpkins and lemons, can be pulled back to see how everything neatly fits together. The detailed petals of calendula are fun to explore with a magnifying glass.

Other flowers that children love to see include pansies (*Viola* spp.), marigolds (*Tagetes* spp.), zinnia

(*Zinnia elegans*), sweet alyssum (*Lobularia maritima*) and portulaca (*Portulaca grandiflora*). The fast-growing stalks and enormous flower heads of sunflowers (*Helianthus annus*) are also visually appealing. Plant a few of these in a sunny location in the back of the children's garden plot. Young gardeners will quickly observe that this is one harvest they can share with feathered friends. Keep your children interested in gardening year round by having them save some seeds for attracting winter birds to their gardens .

Encourage children to observe the variety of sizes and shapes of their plants. Zinnias and marigolds, for example, will appear erect and tall like toy soldiers in a row. Nasturtiums and pansies, on the other hand, will droop or hug the ground, appearing lazy. Compare the round leaves of nasturtiums with the pointed leaves of zinnias. See if your children can find faces in pansies or jaws in snapdragons.

53

Plants to Touch

Children love to explore plants closely, and part of this includes touching them. The perennial lamb's ear (*Stachys byzantina*) and the rose campion (*Lychnis coronaria*) are sensory delights. Both have soft and woolly leaves, just like a lamb's coat. The clammy campion (*Lychnis viscaria*), or catchfly as it is sometimes called, has sticky stems. Of course, children are attracted to anything sticky. While they run their fingers up and down the stem, you can explain that this perennial was once hung upside down to attract flies. They'll be impressed that it was once a natural alternative to chemically treated flypaper. For something unique, try growing hens and chicks (*Sempervivum* spp.). Their succulent cactuslike leaves, arranged in low-growing rosettes, are great fun for small hands to touch.

Other touchable plants include sea pinks (*Armeria maritima*), which have tickly grasslike foliage and small balllike flowers. Because of their compact size, they also grow well in containers. For something a little more out of the ordinary, have your children combine their budding artistic and gardening skills to create an Armeria man. Have them colour a face on a 15-cm (6") clay pot with the sea pink growing in it. Once established, the grassy foliage will resemble a funny haircut.

Plants to Taste

Flowers look pretty, but for young children, munching on fresh garden peas is a sensory delight not to be missed. The 'Homesteader' and 'Green Arrow' cultivars are both sources of sweet-tasting peas, which, because they are heavy producers, will require some staking.

Lettuce is easy and quick to grow in a cooler shadier environment. Under these conditions, one lettuce head will yield several salads. Carrots and radishes are great for the sunnier side of children's gardens. The 'Lady Finger' carrot is small and very tender, so it is well suited to small hands and miniature shovels. A second planting of lettuce, carrots and radishes a few weeks apart will ensure an extended supply. For a colourful addition to summer salads, grow nasturtiums, which have entirely edible leaves and flowers.

Another fun vegetable for children to grow is beans. Many different varieties are available, from the tall-growing pole beans to the small bush types. The compact bush bean 'Bush Blue Lake' is well known for its delicious flavour and, as the name implies, bush form.

Pumpkins are another favourite with children. One to try is 'Jack O Lantern,' perfect for Halloween and great for pies. Because the vines spread quickly, they need ample room to grow. If your space is limited, plant the cultivar 'Jack Be Little.' These tiny pumpkins are only 10 cm (4") across and 6 cm (2.5") high and are ideal for decorating with faces or other works of children's art.

Plants to Smell

Encourage young gardeners to enjoy the fragrance of flowers. From pungent marigolds to sweetly scented sweet peas, from not-so-fragrant bean plants to the eye-watering smell of onions, children's gardens should offer a bouquet of scents for the intrepid young gardener to explore.

Children can make their own charming Armeria man by painting a face on a clay pot and planting armeria in well-drained soil.

SELECTING A SITE

A child's first garden is a special place. Whether you designate a small portion of your own garden or a corner on the other side of the yard, be sure it's in a place where it will succeed. Don't choose a spot you've rejected because the soil is poor or because it's too wet and shady. Ideally, the garden should be near a source of water and away from the roots of large trees.

A garden site that faces south or west and receives about six hours of sunlight per day is ideal for growing most flowers and vegetables. But if you can offer only a shady location, don't despair. Many plants prefer low-light conditions. Even if you live in a townhouse or apartment, your children will still enjoy growing a garden in containers. Both dwarf vegetables and compact flowers are well suited to container growing. To ensure success, help your children select plants that will flourish in your garden's conditions.

GETTING STARTED

Before planting seeds, prepare the children's garden soil. Both clay and sandy soil will benefit from the addition of moist peat moss and compost. Then rake the garden to a smooth surface.

A visit to your local garden centre will reveal an enormous selection of bedding-out plants that are ideal for children's gardens. Provided that the last frost hasn't already surprised you, these can be planted directly in the soil. Be sure to observe the recommended spacing requirements to avoid overcrowding.

It is also a good idea after planting rows of vegetables or flowers to help children label them for easy identification. Use large plastic labels and permanent markers so the labels can withstand rainy days. Even better, put your children's names beside plant names on the labels so they can refer with pride to *their* plants.

CHILDREN'S SUMMER SALAD

1 small head leaf lettuce

1 small red onion, sliced

1 can mandarin orange segments

6 nasturtiums, equal amounts of leaves and flowers

2 tbsp (30 mL) pinenuts

Wash ingredients. Tear lettuce into bite-sized pieces and place in a bowl. Add onion rings, mandarin orange segments and nasturtiums, and sprinkle with pinenuts.

DRESSING

2 tbsp (30 mL) vegetable or canola oil

4 tsp (20 mL) vinegar

1 1/2 – 2 tbsp (22 – 30 mL) orange juice concentrate

1 tbsp (15 mL) sugar or honey

1/2 tsp (5 mL) garlic powder (reduce amount for smaller children

1/2 tsp (5 mL) onion powder (reduce amount for smaller children)

salt and pepper to taste

Mix ingredients and spoon over salad.

Voila! A tasty summer dish that's nutritious, too.

DECORATING CHILDREN'S GARDENS

A sensory garden can be made even more appealing with a variety of surrounding visual elements that extend beyond the plants chosen. If you feel particularly adventurous, you can, for example, help your children paint a small rainbow or other ornament on the fence behind their garden. Or you can ask if they want to use a big bright toy as a garden ornament or planter. Perhaps a small children's bench would also look inviting and encourage them to enjoy a "secret" place all their own. A small plastic birdbath near the bench would allow them to enjoy watching birds close at hand.

Tall sweet peas (*Lathyrus odoratus* 'Spencer Mix') can be used to decorate fences near the children's garden or to create a colourful perfumed teepee using bamboo poles for support. Excellent choices for small containers, such as child-sized wheelbarrows, include the dwarf sweet pea (*Lathyrus odoratus*) cultivars 'Little Sweetheart,' 'Bijou' and 'Knee-Hi.'

For a fun spring project with kids, create a teepee made of tall sweet peas (*Lathyrus odoratus* 'Spencer Mix') or pole beans (*Phaseolus coccineus* 'Scarlet Runner').

Here's what you'll need:

8 long bamboo poles,

1 roll of garden twine,

1 packet of tall sweet peas or scarlet runner beans,

A sunny spot in the garden.

1. Space the bamboo poles about 46 cm (18") apart and push the ends into the ground securely to form a circle 1.25–1.5 M (4–5') in diameter. Leave extra space between two poles for a small doorway.

2. Form a teepee by securing the poles at the top with the garden twine.

3. Starting about 15 cm (6") above the soil surface, tie the twine on one side of the doorway entrance and wrap it around each pole until you reach the other side of the entrance. Secure vertical strands of twine to the horizontal strand at the midpoint between each pair of poles and secure the strands at the top of the teepee. The vertical strands will provide additional support for your peas or beans.

4. Plant your seeds 5 cm (2") deep about every 8–15 cm (3–6") around the perimeter of the teepee except in front of the doorway.

5. Water the freshly planted seeds, and before long you'll have seedlings to care for. Provided that they get regular water and plenty of sun, the plants will cover the bamboo poles with lots of cheerful flowers and, if you've chosen pole beans, lots of delicious beans.

CARING FOR CHILDREN'S GARDENS

Although you shouldn't fret too much if some flowers succumb to infestations of aphids or mildew, you can help prevent their occurrence by establishing a routine maintenance schedule that includes watering, weeding, deadheading and looking for unusual spotting, discolouration and webbing—all signs of insect infestations or disease.

Teaching garden care to your children is important to nurturing their sense of responsibility, but never force the issue. Too many adults had their love of gardening stifled because they were forced into gardening regimes as children without understanding their value. Help your children learn that healthy plants are better able to defend themselves against diseases and pests and that good air circulation and sanitation can go a long way toward minimizing their threat.

Children, who are far from squeamish, don't see all insects as pests, and they're right not to. The lovely ladybug, for example, enjoys feasting on aphids, and children of all ages thrill at watching a ladybug crawl up a shirtsleeve. Young gardeners can quickly appreciate that chemicals used to control aphids might also harm their favourite ladybugs, bees or butterflies. Their curiosity can be a starting point for learning about environmentally benign ways to deal with unwanted critters in the garden. Chemically free gardens are safer havens for children, plants and ladybugs alike, and will go a long way toward instilling in youngsters a desire to nurture their gardens.

BRINGING THE SENSORY GARDEN INDOORS

Bring fun learning experiences indoors with a few projects that take just minutes of preparation. The cut-off tops of carrots, beets and parsnips, when placed in a saucer of water, will begin to sprout in a few days. By watching such experiments, children will quickly discover the importance of regular water to plants.

A similar experiment involves cutting a leafy stalk of celery lengthwise, halfway up, starting at the root end. Place one leg of the celery stalk in a glass of water dyed with blue food colouring and the other leg in water coloured red. Young gardeners will be able to trace the route of the water up the stalk by observing each of the coloured veins.

Outdoor and indoor gardening projects should all be geared to cultivating a love of nature in your children. As you go through the process of designing, planting and enjoying the harvest from your children's garden, consider taking photographs or videos. Mount photos in your youngsters' own garden journal, or designate a children's garden video, so that together you can savour the fun times had in your children's special sensory garden.

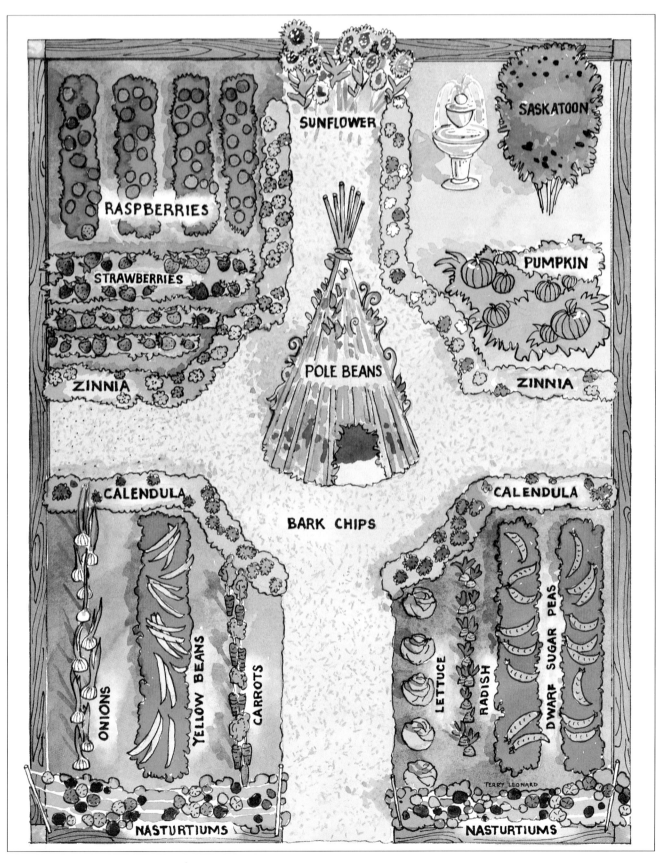

This exquisite children's garden will thrill children's senses with edible vegetables and fruit, fast-growing calendula and nasturtiums, sunflowers to touch and taste and a pole bean teepee to play in.

THE CHILDREN'S GARDEN

COMMON NAME	BOTANICAL NAME	HEIGHT	SPREAD
Perennials			
Hollyhocks	*Althaea rosea*	2 M (7')	25–30 cm (10–12")
Sea Pinks	*Armeria maritima*	10–30 cm (4–12")	10–30 cm (4–12")
Painted Daisy	*Chrysanthemum coccineum*	30–60 cm (12–24")	30–45 cm (12–18")
Daisy	*Chrysanthemum x superbum*	30–90 cm (12–36")	30–90 cm (12–36")
Rose Campion	*Lychnis coronaria*	60–90 cm (24–36")	30–40 cm (12–16")
Clammy Campion	*Lychnis viscaria*	30 cm (12")	30 cm (12")
Hens and Chicks	*Sempervivum* spp.	2.5–10 cm (1–4")	15–30 cm (6–12")
Lamb's Ears	*Stachys byzantina*	30–40 cm (12–16")	30–40 cm (12–16")
Annuals			
Snapdragon	*Antirrhinum majus*	10–60 cm (4–24")	varies
Calendula	*Calendula officinalis*	12–60 cm (5–24")	12–30 cm (5–12")
Sunflower	*Helianthus annus*	45 cm–3 M (1.5–10')	30–45 cm (12–18")
Dwarf Sweet Pea	*Lathyrus odoratus* 'Bijou'	30 cm (12")	15–30 cm (6–12")
Dwarf Sweet Pea	*Lathyrus odoratus* 'Knee-Hi'	30 cm (12")	15–30 cm (6–12")
Dwarf Sweet Pea	*Lathyrus odoratus* 'Little Sweetheart'	30 cm (12")	15–30 cm (6–12")
Tall Sweet Pea	*Lathyrus odoratus* 'Spencer Mix'	3 M (10')	5–15 cm (2–6")
Sweet Alyssum	*Lobularia maritima*	5–10 cm (2–4")	25 cm (10")
Portulaca	*Portulaca grandiflora*	5–8 cm (2–3")	30 cm (12")
Marigold	*Tagetes* spp.	10–70 cm (4–28")	varies
Nasturtium	*Tropaeolum majus*	15–60 cm (6–24")	15–60 cm (6–24")
Pansy	*Viola* spp.	10–15 cm (4–6")	varies
Zinnia	*Zinnia elegans*	12–60 cm (5–24")	12 cm (5")
Vegetables			
Carrot	*Daucus carota* var. *sativus* 'Baby Spike'	10 cm (4")	varies
Carrot	*Daucus carota* var. *sativus* 'Lady Finger'	5 cm (2")	varies
Carrot	*Daucus carota* var. *sativus* 'Thumbelina'	1–5 cm (.5–2")	varies
Miniature Pumpkin	*Cucurbita pepo* 'Jack Be Little'	30 cm (12")	varies
Pumpkin	*Cucurbita pepo* 'Jack O Lantern'	45 cm (18")	varies
Head Lettuce	*Lactuca sativa* 'Buttercrunch'	15 cm (6")	15 cm (6")
Leaf Lettuce	*Lactuca sativa* 'Prize Head'	20 cm (8")	15 cm (6")
Pea	*Lathyrus* 'Green Arrow'	1 M (3')	25 cm (10")
Pea	*Lathyrus* 'Homesteader'	1 M (3')	25 cm (10")
Edible Pod Pea	*Lathyrus* 'Oregon Giant'	75 cm (30")	25 cm (10")
Pole Bean	*Phaseolus coccineus* 'Scarlet Runner'	3 M (10')	15 cm (6")
Bush Bean	*Phaseolus vulgaris* 'Bush Blue Lake'	45 cm (18")	45 cm (18")
Radish	*Raphanus sativus* 'French Breakfast'	15 cm (6")	2.5 cm (1")
Radish	*Raphanus sativus* 'Sparkler'	15 cm (6")	2.5 cm (1")
Shrubs and Others			
Smoky Saskatoon	*Amelanchier alnifolia* 'Smoky'	3 M (10')	2 M (7')
Strawberry	*Fragaria* 'Tristar'	10 cm (4")	varies
Raspberry	*Rubus* 'Boyne'	1–1.5 M (3–5')	varies

FOLIAGE COLOUR	FLOWER COLOUR	COMMENTS
green	wide variety	bright colours, needs staking
green	magenta pink	grassy leaves with pom-pomlike blooms
green	pinks	nice cut blooms, attracts butterflies
green	white	cheerful blooms, attracts butterflies
silver grey	carmine pink	soft leaves, bright colours, fun to touch
green	rose pink	sticky stems, good interest plant
varies	pink, white	interesting texture, reproduces quickly
silver grey	dull white	soft woolly leaves, fun to touch
green	wide variety	cheerful colours, fun flower
green	orange, yellow	bright colours, attractive in containers
green	yellow	bright colour, attracts birds and insects
green	wide variety	scented, bright colours, nice cut flower
green	wide variety	scented, bright colours, nice cut flower
green	wide variety	scented, bright colours, nice cut flower
green	wide variety	scented, bright colours, nice cut flower
green	rose, purple, white	scented long-lasting blooms
green	wide variety	dazzling colours, blooms open on sunny days
green	orange, yellow	bright colours
green	orange, yellow	scented, both blooms and foliage edible
green	wide variety	cheerful colours with facelike patterns
green	wide variety	cheerful colours, nice cut flower
green	not applicable	edible root, good cultivar for containers
green	not applicable	edible root, good cultivar for containers
green	not applicable	edible golf ball-shaped roots
green	yellow	miniature size, fun plant
green	yellow	suitable for carving
green	white	edible leaves, blooms late in season
purple	white	attractive edible leaves, blooms late in season
green	yellow, white	sweet-flavoured peas
green	yellow, white	sweet-flavoured peas
green	white	edible pods
green	scarlet red	attractive blooms, edible beans
green	white	compact cultivar, edible beans
green	not applicable	piquant flavour, fast from seed
green	not applicable	piquant flavour, fast from seed
green	white	juicy delicious fruit
green	white	all-season fruit
green	not applicable	sweet-tasting fruit

CHAPTER

6

THE CUTTING GARDEN

"Only the flower sanctifies the vase"

–Joshua Sylvester

Flowers are for pleasure, pure and simple. And for those who love flowers, nothing is more pleasurable than cutting bouquets of cheerful scented blooms that bring a touch of nature indoors. Many annuals, perennials, herbs, bulbs, vines and ornamental grasses, in an enormous range of colours, are suitable for cutting. Many gardeners begin by snipping the odd beautiful bloom and long to go further but hesitate for fear of mutilating their cherished and carefully designed gardens. To explore the art of flower arranging further, they need to develop cutting gardens.

Cutting gardens can double as display gardens. Luscious white, pink and red peonies bloom in unison with flame-coloured lilies, offering a bounty of beautiful blooms also appropriate for cutting.

KINDS OF CUTTING GARDENS

A cutting garden, from the floral arranger's point of view, is one whose main purpose is to provide flowers for indoor enjoyment. Large appetites for cut flowers can be appeased with production cutting gardens. In these, favourite flowers, carefully chosen for colour, foliage or form, are grown inexpensively in rows, like carrots and lettuce. Perennial everlastings, such as versatile statice or airy baby's breath, can also be grown in the cutting garden and dried for indoor bouquets. The cutting garden is also an ideal place to transplant withered tulips once their foliage has died down. Later, in the autumn, they may be returned to the spring garden spot where they are most enjoyed.

If your space is limited, a display garden that harmonizes with your overall garden design can also offer a variety of flowers for cutting purposes. Informal island beds that double as cutting gardens, for instance, can be incorporated into existing garden areas. If a more formal look is preferred, a symmetrically arranged dual purpose garden can be created. Or you might consider an attractive combination of beds, separated by brick pathways, to reinforce the architectural lines of your house. Note that in display gardens also serving as cutting gardens, individual flowers must be cut somewhat judiciously so that large gaps are not left behind to affect the appearance of the display.

SELECTING A SITE

Cutting gardens can be any size, as long as you can walk or reach into all parts of them. When selecting a site, keep in mind that for the largest harvest of beautiful blooms, the place you choose will need at least six hours of sunlight per day. However, if your only choice happens to be shady, a good selection of shade-tolerant flowers is still available. Remember, the key to success in any specialty garden is selecting flowers that will flourish in the conditions you have to offer, so be certain to study the cultural requirements of all your selections before planting them. A wise gardener works with nature, not against it.

SOIL

Soil is the one requirement for growing flowers that is the most amenable to change. Peat moss, compost and well-aged manure will assist you in amending most less-than-perfect soil conditions. Generally, well-drained organically rich soil is suitable for cutting gardens, but if you are uncertain about the quality of your soil, it may be advisable to have a professional soil test done before you plant.

DESIGNING THE CUTTING GARDEN

If your appetite for cut flowers is large, you may wish to go the route of a production garden, in which case basic principles of design are of little consequence. What you want is simply easy access to rows of healthy plants. An ideal location for such a production garden might be a sunny unused side yard or a corner of your yard not completely visible from main traffic areas. If your yard space is small, then turn to a display garden, in which case all the usual considerations of garden design apply. If it can be viewed from all directions, place the tallest flowers in the centre, the mid-sized ones in the middle and the shortest ones in front to complete a well-balanced composition.

Cutting garden layouts should allow for flower beds arranged in rows at least 2 M (6') long and divided into blocks measuring 60 x 90 cm (2 x 3'). If you choose, single rows and blocks can then be combined into creative patterns. Pathways between areas can be mulched with bark chips to help keep your shoes clean and allow easy access for watering, weeding and harvesting your blooms.

Cut lavish bouquets of flowers from colourful gardens of sun-loving cosmos and yarrow. Both plants are ideal for less-than-perfect soil conditions.

To maximize the amount of sunlight cutting garden flowers receive, position the tallest plants in the back row, which is ideally to the north so they won't leave shorter flowers in the shade. Then decrease the heights of the plants until the shortest are located in the southernmost row. Plants of similar heights should be planted in north-south rows to reduce shadows. Keep in mind

This cactus-flowered dahlia will add vibrant colour to your cutting garden. Choose from many available forms and colours.

that good air circulation is important for healthy plants. To avoid overcrowding, consider the mature size of each flower species and space accordingly.

To simplify maintenance, group plants according to their cultural requirements. For example, if you are growing annuals and perennials, try to plant the annuals together so they can be cleaned up easily in the autumn. You should also consider grouping drought tolerant plants so that precious water can be distributed to the more demanding varieties.

To enjoy a continual supply of cut flowers, select a range of plants that bloom at different times through-

out the season. Favourite cut flowers can be enjoyed over a longer period if you stage planting times two or three weeks apart rather than sowing all the seeds at once. Provided that they are suitable for your location, spring blooming tulips and daffodils can also be included.

Plan your selections with a view toward their eventual arrangements within your home. You'll need an interesting variety of colours, forms and textures to create artful compositions—formal or informal, contemporary or nostalgic. Some gardeners prefer colours that quietly harmonize with interiors; others prefer bold accents. Whatever your choices, work with the interior design of your home, not against it. To plan for a medley of textures and forms, consider planting delphiniums (*Delphinium* spp.) and colourful gladioli (*Gladiolus* spp.) for vertical accents and the low-growing baby's breath (*Gypsophila paniculata*) or sneezewort (*Achillea ptarmica* 'The Pearl') for their delicate airy appearance.

MAINTENANCE
Watering

Cutting gardens require the same kind of maintenance as other flower beds. Water needs will vary with the kind of plant, the climate and the soil. Avoid, however, frequent light waterings as these encourage the development of shallow feeder roots, which make plants more vulnerable to drought. Deep watering, on the other hand, will encourage the plant roots to grow downward in search of moisture.

Water your cutting garden early in the morning to reduce fungal disease and evaporation. A shallow depression around the base of the flowers, either individually or as one long row, will help retain water near the root system. This is especially effective if your cutting garden is on a slope. Trickle irrigation systems are very effective and easily attached to outdoor taps. Soaker hoses placed beside the row will also deliver water directly to the soil, where the flowers can best use it.

Staking

Inevitably, some flower varieties will require staking. To stake your flowers, insert 60–90 cm (2–3') stakes at the back of each flowering stem and secure loosely with green ties or jute twine. For longer rows of cut flowers, insert larger stakes at the ends of rows and smaller stakes every few feet. Then link the stakes with twine. This additional support will make cutting bouquets easier.

Weeding

"A weed is a plant whose virtues have not yet been discovered," noted a wise gardener a century ago. You may toil all weekend pulling weeds and daubing the sweat from your brow, but come Monday evening, when you visit your garden with a cool drink in hand, the weeds are back—little armies of them infiltrating your hard-won piece of paradise. With or without virtues, weeds are tough survivors. They will compete for nutrients, water and light, and if you let them they will overwhelm your lovely flowers and turn the garden into a tangle of rank prickly growth.

With those encouraging words in mind, I offer this advice: managing weeds is a necessary part of gardening. You can make the task more palatable if you think of weeding as an opportunity to appreciate the qualities of your flowers close at hand. A thorough weeding once a week is usually sufficient for most cutting gardens, but if they are large, you may wish to make the task more bearable by weeding a small portion each day. The task may also be more enjoyable if you incorporate it into the time you spend cutting flowers. Regardless of your approach, removing weeds while they are small will prevent them from going to seed.

Deadheading

Another incidental chore that keeps the garden looking attractive is *deadheading*—that is, the removal of spent flowers. Deadheading both annuals and perennials regularly will ensure a healthy succession of blooms. To deadhead, use flower shears to cut back soft-stemmed plants to just above a pair of leaves. Or you may cut just above the dormant bud on a stem or in a leaf axil (the point where the leaf joins the stem). This encourages plants to grow bushier and, in most cases, to produce more flowers. Keep in mind that when you deadhead tulips, the foliage must be left in place until it yellows and dries so that it can nourish the bulb.

Controlling Pests and Diseases

A well-tended flower garden, one that offers optimum conditions for growth, will have fewer pests and diseases than a garden of undernourished flowers and exhausted soil. But even gardens growing in ideal conditions require regular inspection to keep serious insect infestations at bay. Closely examine the leaf axils and the undersides of leaves for pests and eggs. Watch for discolouring of leaves, leaf curling or wilting, holes in the flower buds and flowers that are flecked and spotted. All are indications of insect damage. If problems arise turn to your local garden centre for help in identifying the pest before attempting corrective measures. Above all, practice good sanitation. Keep the flower garden free of the debris that insects find attractive.

Plant disease symptoms include stunting yellowed leaves, premature leaf fall, brown fuzzy patches, soft mushy areas and a general decline in vigour. As soon as any symptom is noticed, remove the affected plant parts and dispose of them in the garbage. Do not put this debris into the compost pile as diseased organisms can infect the compost. Sterilize your cutting tools in a bleach solution before cutting anything else in the garden.

CUTTING FLOWERS

The time of day that flowers are cut is important to their longevity in an arrangement. Some gardeners prefer the early morning, others the early evening, and both have advantages. Flowers cut in the early morning, before the dew evaporates, will require less conditioning because the flower tissues are well supplied with water. Blooms cut in the early evening take advantage of high sugar reserves produced throughout the day, which will maintain freshness until conditioning takes place. This is especially helpful if your arrangements are destined for competitions and must be very long lived.

When handling fresh-cut flowers, hold them by the stem to avoid damaging blossoms and foliage. Flower stems should be cut with a clean sharp blade. Dull tools can crush or damage the vital water-carrying capillaries so invest in quality cutting tools that will keep a sharp edge. Flower shears are ideal for cutting most soft stems.

Deciding what to cut means paying attention to both the blossom and the stem. Only the perfect blossoms will do for indoor arrangements because flowers damaged by insects, disease or inclement weather will not lend themselves to aesthetically pleasing arrangements. Flowers that are starting to droop also don't contribute to pleasing arrangements because they will have a short vase life. To allow for the greatest creative latitude in designing floral arrangements, cut the longest stems possible. Later, indoors, you can recut for shorter stems.

A flower-gathering basket is picturesque, but a clean bucket of tepid water is much kinder to most

Lilies create a dazzling midsummer display. When cutting for indoor bouquets, remove the pollen-bearing anthers.

freshly cut flowers. Place every stem in water immediately after cutting and keep the pail out of direct sunlight. A few flowers will need immediate special attention. Daffodils, for example, should be placed in their own pail of water as their sap can harm other flowers. Other plants, such as lilies, can harm your clothes and furniture. Remove their pollen-bearing anthers to prevent stains.

PRECONDITIONING AND SPECIAL TREATMENTS

Flower arrangements will look fresher and last longer if they have been *conditioned*, a process sometimes called *hardening*. Conditioning involves filling flower and leaf tissues to capacity with water.

Some flowers require special treatment before they are conditioned or they will not absorb water effectively. Poppies and hollyhocks, for example, contain a milky or sticky sap that oozes from their stems when they are cut. To prevent nutrients from being lost with this sap, the ends of the stems must be sealed immediately. Do this by holding the stem ends over a candle flame until they blacken or by dipping them—approximately 1 cm (.5")—in boiling water for at least 30 seconds. Take precautions to ensure that the heat doesn't damage the foliage or blossoms. Flowers with woody stems, such as chrysanthemums, also require special treatment before conditioning. With a sharp short-bladed knife, make a 2.5–7.5 cm (1–3") split up from the base of the stem. Then split it crosswise to expose even more water-absorbing surface. Some gardeners advocate pulverizing the ends with a hammer to achieve the same purpose. This may increase absorption at first, but the crushed tissues become quickly suscepti-

Announcing the summer solstice, oriental poppies burst into bloom with silken petals surrounding purple-black stamens. Immediately after cutting, sear their stem ends over a candle flame to prevent loss of nutrients.

ble to bacterial decay. Daffodils exude toxins that are harmful to other plants, so place daffodils in a separate vase for at least one hour before arranging them with other flowers.

Some flowers, such as delphiniums, have hollow stems. These need to have their stems filled with water before conditioning. To do this, turn the stems upside down, fill them with cool water and plug them with a small piece of cotton batting or absorbent floral foam. Sometimes tiny air bubbles become trapped in the stems and impede the water flow. To eliminate these, pierce the stems with a pin just below the flower head. Immerse the plugged stem ends in boiling water for about twenty seconds to seal them, and then transfer the flowers to a container of tepid water for conditioning. This special treatment ensures the longevity of these dramatic vertical accents in your arrangements.

For fast impromptu arrangements, recutting the stems under water will maximize freshness and vase life. For some flowers this minimum treatment will be adequate. Immerse only the stem ends under a running faucet or in a water-filled sink or basin and then simply recut the stems on an angle, which allows them to absorb more water when resting on the bottom of the vase. Avoid exposing the stem ends to air at any point in this process to ensure that air bubbles do not lodge in the stem.

CONDITIONING

Once you have completed recutting the stems and performing other special treatments, the conditioning process can begin. Immerse the cut stems loosely in a clean container of tepid water. Galvanized metal containers are available at garden centres and boutiques, but a plastic household pail works just fine.

With asterlike flowers, fleabane is an excellent cut flower for informal arrangements. Available in mauve, pink, purple and blue, this perennial prefers full sun and well-drained soil.

Floral preservatives can be added to both the conditioning water and the vase water as can floral additives, which inhibit bacterial growth while supplying life-sustaining sugars. Preservatives and additives are readily available at garden centres and are an easy alternative to recutting stems and changing water regularly.

Leave the recut flowers in a cool dark place for several hours or overnight. Darkness causes the tiny pores in the leaves and stems to close, reducing moisture loss. The next morning, cut the stems once more under water and remove foliage below the new waterline. This is especially necessary for some marigolds, calendulas, asters, stocks, dahlias, dusty millers and zinnias as their leaves decay rapidly when submerged.

ARRANGING FLOWERS

Flower arranging is a purely personal affair. But bear in mind that the design principles of balance, rhythm and proportion, and colour, texture and form apply as much to arrangements in vases as to arrangements in gardens. Generally, combining three or five of one colour or plant type in arrangements creates a more artful effect, but don't overlook the simple and obvious: sometimes the most stunning statement is made by a single perfect bloom floating in a bowl of water.

If flower arranging becomes more than casual entertainment, you may consider showing your arrangements at floral exhibitions. There, flower arrangements are awarded marks for various qualities including condition, form, stem, foliage, colour and size of blooms. Uniformity, proper maturity, freedom from bruises and blemishes, and clarity and brilliance of colour are also considered. Contact your horticultural society or garden club for information about local floral exhibitions.

Here are some lovely combinations of spring and summer flowers for creating lavish bouquets and arrangements:

1. Small glass bowls of dainty lily-of-the-valley.

2. Blue pansies and white perennial candytuft.

3. Yellow primroses and orange pansies.

4. Pink peonies, roses and stocks, blue clematis and baby's breath.

5. Magenta Asiatic lilies, gay-feather, painted daisies and delphiniums.

6. Cosmos, pink lavatera, larkspur and white and mauve sweet peas.

7. Yellow calendula, fernleaf yarrow and painted tongue.

8. Mauve-blue nigella, larkspur, yellow Iceland poppies and white sweet peas.

9. Pink and white snapdragons, blue delphiniums, pink clematis and rosy-pink clarkia.

10. Yellow hybrid lilies and white baby's breath.

DRYING FLOWERS

Dried flowers remind us of the splendour of our summer gardens long after they lie buried deep under snow. For this reason they have become enormously popular and are now featured items at many florist shops and gardening centres. But there is still something deeply satisfying about creating your own permanent reminder of summer.

Perennial baby's breath, in masses of tiny white flowers, enjoys sunny locations and well-drained soil. Its delicate blooms enhance both fresh and dried arrangements.

Extend an invitation to butterflies with the tall spikes of gayfeather. This showy perennial is excellent in fresh and dried arrangements.

Many annuals and a good selection of perennials are suitable for drying and arranging. The best results for some are obtained through air drying while others require silica gel drying. To air dry flowers simply strip the leaves, tie the stems in small bunches and hang them upside down in a dark dry place with good air circulation. To prepare flowers for drying in silica gel (available in many garden and craft centres), stand them in water for a few hours to firm the petals, and then cut the stems to about 2.5 cm (1") in length. Stand the stems in a 2.5-cm- (1") thick layer of silica gel in the bottom of an airtight container and continue filling the container until the blooms are completely covered. Seal the container and put it in a warm dry place. Drying will take about one week for most flowers.

Some excellent choices for air drying include calendula (*Calendula officinalis*), celosia (*Celosia argentea* var. *cristata*), larkspur (*Delphinium* spp.), strawflower (*Helichrysum* spp.), money plant (*Lunaria annua*), peony (*Paeonia* spp.) and love-in-a-mist (*Nigella* spp.). Silica gel will be the preferred method of drying for snapdragons (*Antirrhinum majus*), clarkia (*Clarkia amoena*), dahlia (*Dahlia pinnata*), painted tongue (*Salpiglossis sinuata*), delphinium (*Delphinium* spp.) and foxglove (*Digitalis grandiflora*).

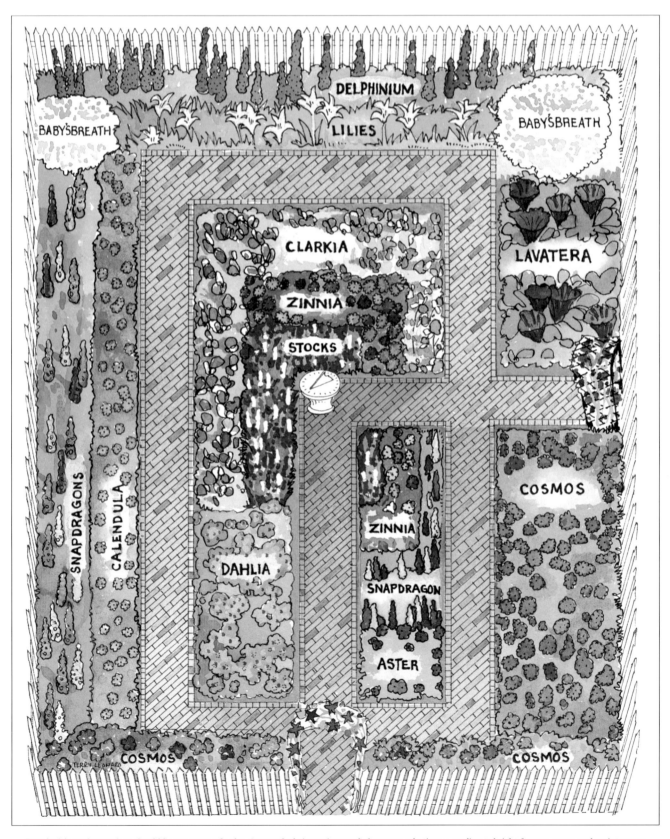

Even lavish cutting gardens should have a sense of order. Arrange beds in sections and plant your selections according to height for easy access and maintenance. The straight lines of this cutting garden are practical as well as artistic.

THE CUTTING GARDEN

COMMON NAME	BOTANICAL NAME	HEIGHT	SPREAD
Annuals			
Snapdragon	*Antirrhinum majus*	15–60 cm (6–24")	varies
Calendula	*Calendula officinalis*	12–60 cm (5–24")	12–30 cm (5–12")
China Aster	*Callistephus chinensis*	15–60 cm (6–24")	15–60 cm (6–24")
Celosia	*Celosia argentea* var. *cristata*	15–20 cm (6–8")	10–15 cm (4–6")
Clarkia	*Clarkia amoena*	30–60 cm (12–24")	30–40 cm (12–16")
Chrysanthemum	*Chrysanthemum morifolium*	40–60 cm (16–24")	varies
Cosmos	*Cosmos bipinnatus*	40 cm–1 M (16–36")	20–40 cm (8–16")
Annual Dahlia	*Dahlia pinnata*	15–60 cm (6–24")	30–40 cm (12–16")
Larkspur	*Delphinium* spp.	45 cm–1.5 M (1.5–5')	30 cm (12")
Dusty Miller	many genera & species	varies	varies
Strawflower	*Helichrysum* spp.	45–90 cm (18–36")	30–45 cm (12–18")
Dwarf Sweet Pea	*Lathyrus odoratus* 'Knee-Hi'	15–30 cm (6–12")	15 cm (6")
Tall Sweet Pea	*Lathyrus odoratus* 'Spencer Mix'	3 M (10')	5–15 cm (2–6")
Lavatera	*Lavatera trimestris*	1 M (3')	30–40 cm (12–16")
Annual Statice	*Limonium sinuatum*	30–60 cm (12–24")	30–40 cm (12–16")
Money Plant	*Lunaria annua*	45–60 cm (18–24")	30–40 cm (12–16")
Stocks	*Matthiola incana*	25–50 cm (10–20")	15–20 cm (6–8")
Silver Feather Grass	*Miscanthus sinensis* 'Silberfeder'	1.5 M (5')	1 M (3')
Nicotiana	*Nicotiana* spp.	15 cm–1 M (6–36")	varies
Love-in-a-Mist	*Nigella* spp.	60–90 cm (24–36")	30 cm (12")
Fountain Grass	*Pennisetum alopecuriodes*	60–90 cm (24–36")	50–75 cm (20–30")
Painted Tongue	*Salpiglossis sinuata*	30–45 cm (12–18")	15–20 cm (6–8")
Butterfly Flower	*Schizanthus* x *wisetonensis*	30–60 cm (12–24")	20 cm (8")
Marigold	*Tagetes* spp.	10–70 cm (4–28")	10–30 cm (4–12")
Zinnia	*Zinnia elegans*	12–60 cm (5–24")	12–30 cm (5–12")
Perennials			
Fernleaf Yarrow	*Achillea filipendulina*	1–1.3 M (3–4')	60 cm (24")
Common Yarrow	*Achillea millefolium*	45–60 cm (18–24")	45–60 cm (18–24")
Sneezewort	*Achillea ptarmica* 'The Pearl'	45–60 cm (18–24")	45–60 cm (18–24")
Hollyhock	*Althaea rosea*	2 M (7')	25–30 cm (10–12")
Golden Marguerite	*Anthemis tinctoria*	60 cm (24")	30–45 cm (12–18")
Columbine	*Aquilegia* spp.	30–60 cm (12–24")	30–60 cm (12–24")
Artemisia	*Artemisia* spp.	20–60 cm (8–24")	varies
Bulbous Oat Grass	*Arrhenatherum elatius* var. *bulbosum* 'Variegatum'	30–45 cm (12–18")	30 cm (12")
Astilbe	*Astilbe* spp.	30–60 cm (12–24")	30–60 cm (12–24")
Quaking Grass	*Briza maxima*	30–60 cm (12–24")	30 cm (12")
Peachleaf Bellflower	*Campanula persicifolia*	75 cm (30")	30–45 cm (12–18")
Painted Daisy	*Chrysanthemum coccineum*	30–60 cm (12–24")	30–45 cm (12–18")
Lily-of-the-Valley	*Convallaria majalis*	10–20 cm (4–8")	varies
Delphinium	*Delphinium* spp.	60 cm–2 M (2–7')	25–50 cm (10–20")
Bleeding Heart	*Dicentra* spp.	30–90 cm (12–36")	30–60 cm (12–24")
Foxglove	*Digitalis grandiflora*	60 cm (24")	30–45 cm (12–18")
Globe Thistle	*Echinops ritro*	1 M (3')	1 M (3')
Sea Holly	*Eryngium* spp.	60–90 cm (24–36")	varies
Cypress Spurge	*Euphorbia cyparissis*	30 cm (12")	30–60 cm (12–24")
Blanketflower	*Gaillardia aristata*	30–90 cm (12–36")	30–45 cm (12–18")
Baby's Breath	*Gypsophila paniculata*	1 M (3')	1 M (3')

FOLIAGE COLOUR	FLOWER COLOUR	COMMENTS
green	wide variety	long-lasting blooms, vertical accent
green	orange, yellow	bright flowers on long stems
green	pink, blue, purple, white	nice compact blooms, cool colour range
green	wide variety	unusual flower shapes and vivid colours, everlasting
green	rose, pink, purple, white	delicate, satiny petals
green	wide variety	late summer colour
green	magenta, pink, white	airy sprays of daisy blooms
green	wide variety	many flower forms available
green	pink, blue, mauve, white	attractive vertical accent
silver grey	yellow	grown for foliage colour
green	wide variety	everlasting, pick before full blown
green	wide variety	scented, bright colours, nice cut flower
green	wide variety	scented, bright colours, nice cut flower
green	pink, white	glistening blooms, strong, upright stems
green	wide variety	bright colours, everlasting
green	purple, white	dollar-size seed pods, everlasting
green	pink, blue, purple, white	very fragrant, vertical accent
green	inconspicuous	silvery white, shimmery plumes, good accent
green	wide variety	evening scented blooms, attractive vertical accent
green	blue, purple, white	unusual, delicate bloom and seed pod, everlasting
green	inconspicuous	buff-coloured feathery spikes
green	warm earth tones	softens arrangements
green	wide variety	soft colours, interesting flower shape
green	orange, yellow	bright colours
green	wide variety	many flower forms available, good in informal arrangements
green	yellow	bright colour, long-lasting blooms
green	carmine, pink, ivory	bright colour, long-lasting blooms
green	white	softens arrangements, used as filler
green	wide variety	bright colours, needs staking
green	yellow	bright colour
green	wide variety	unusual flower forms
silver grey	yellow	attractive foliage
green, cream	tan	unique vertical accent
green	wide variety	soft, airy blooms
green	inconspicuous	graceful clusters of heart-shaped seed pods
green	blue, white	delicate bell-shaped blooms
green	magenta , pink	bright cheerful colours
green	white	scented, delicate bell-shaped blooms
green	pink, blue, mauve, white	strong vertical accent
green	pink, white	heart-shaped blooms on graceful arching branches
green	yellow	showy vertical accent
blue green	blue	unusual flower heads, everlasting blooms
blue green	blue grey	unusual flower, everlasting, pick when fully open
green	greenish yellow	unusual coloured bracts
green	red, orange, yellow, maroon	cheerful daisy flower
green	white	delicate array of blooms, everlasting

COMMON NAME	BOTANICAL NAME	HEIGHT	SPREAD
Perennials continued			
False Heliopsis	*Heliopsis scabra*	1 M (3')	1 M (3')
Hosta	*Hosta* spp.	30–90 cm (12–36")	varies
Perennial Candytuft	*Iberis sempervirens*	30 cm (12")	30–50 cm (12–20")
Siberian Iris	*Iris sibirica*	60 cm–1.2 M (2–4')	varies
Spike Gayfeather	*Liatris spicata*	45 cm (18")	30 cm (12")
Sea Lavender	*Limonium latifolium*	60 cm (24")	30–45 cm (12–18")
German Statice	*Limonium tartaricum*	45–60 cm (18–24")	45–60 cm (18–24")
Ostrich Fern	*Matteuccia struthiopteris*	1 M–1.5 M (3–5')	varies
Bee Balm	*Monarda didyma*	60–90 cm (24–36")	60 cm (24")
Peony	*Paeonia* spp.	varies	varies
Iceland Poppy	*Papaver nudicaule*	30–40 cm (12–16")	30–40 cm (12–16")
Oriental Poppy	*Papaver orientale*	30–90 cm (12–36")	30–90 cm (12–36")
Canary Grass	*Phalaris canariensis*	1 M (3')	varies
Primrose	*Primula* spp.	varies	varies
Coneflower	*Rudbeckia laciniata* var. *flore-pleno*	1–1.5 M (3–5')	1 M (3')
Goldenrod	*Solidago* spp.	1–1.5 M (3–5')	1–1.5 M (3–5')
Globeflower	*Trollius* spp.	40–90 cm (16–36")	25–50 cm (10–20")
Spike Speedwell	*Veronica spicata*	45–60 cm (18–24")	30 cm (12")
Viola	*Viola* spp.	5–15 cm (2–6")	varies
Bulbs and Others			
Blue Globe Onion	*Allium caeruleum*	60 cm (24")	varies
Tuberous Begonia	*Begonia* x *tuberhybrida*	20–45 cm (8–18")	20–25 cm (8–10")
Fritillaria	*Fritillaria pallidiflora*	30–45 cm (12–18")	varies
Gladioli	*Gladiolus* spp.	45 cm–1 M (24–36")	10–15 cm (4–6")
Bearded Iris	*Iris* x *germanica*	varies	varies
Asiatic Lily	*Lilium* spp.	45 cm–1 M (24–36")	varies
Daffodil	*Narcissus* spp.	15–45 cm (6–18")	varies
Tulip	*Tulipa* spp.	5–60 cm (2–24")	varies

FOLIAGE COLOUR	FLOWER COLOUR	COMMENTS
green	yellow	bright colour, long-lasting blooms
yellow, green, blue, white	mauve, white	leaf and flower useful in arrangements
green	white	scented, delicate blooms
green	blue, purple, white	striking colours and flower form
green	rosy purple	dramatic vertical accent, blooms open from top to bottom
green	lavender blue	good in dried arrangements
green	silver grey	good in dried arrangements
green	none	softens arrangements, useful foliage
green	red, mauve, white	scented blooms, unusual flower heads
green	wide variety	outstanding large blooms, some cultivars scented
green	pink, orange, yellow, white	pick when buds begin to open
green	red, pink, salmon, white	decorative seed heads, pick when buds begin to open
green	inconspicuous	delicate accent
green	wide variety	small delicate blooms, some scented
green	yellow	cheerful daisy flower, long-lasting blooms
green	yellow	vertical accent, soft yellow plumes, everlasting
green	orange, yellow	bright colour, long-lasting
green	pink, blue, white	good vertical accent
green	wide variety	cheerful spring flower
green	blue	attractive globe flower
green	wide variety	variety of flower forms
blue green	mint green	striking blooms, dramatic accent
green	wide variety	dramatic vertical accent
green	wide variety	rainbow of colours
green	wide variety	dramatic display, remove pollen-bearing anthers
green	pink, orange, yellow, cream, white	cut when bud begins to open
green	wide variety	bloom follows light, pick just before opening

THE ROSE GARDEN

"A rose is a rose is a rose"

–Gertrude Stein

The sumptuous rose has long been proclaimed by gardeners as the Queen of Flowers. The Chinese philosopher Confucius wrote of delicate roses in the Imperial Gardens five hundred years before the birth of Christ. Most modern-day roses trace their heritage to these and roses grown in Japan.

Rose growing was a thriving industry in the ancient world. As conquering armies moved back and forth across medieval frontiers, new varieties were brought home to adorn palatial gardens. The Greeks and Persians cultivated roses extensively for their beauty, exotic perfumes and purported medicinal qualities. In prestigious and noble homes, rose petals were used to delicately shower guests and cover pathways. Wreaths and garlands of roses had a place of honour in festivals and were exchanged as symbols of love at weddings.

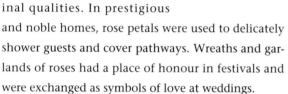

Against a dark green backdrop, this hybrid rose provides an impressive colourful display.

The romance with roses increased dramatically in the late eighteenth century with the introduction of Chinese varieties to Europe. The rose's popularity was given an additional boost by the Empress Josephine of France, who was determined to collect all known varieties in her cherished gardens at Chateau Malmaison. She encouraged her drawing master, Pierre Joseph Redouté, to take up botanical illustration and he subsequently left us a stunning pictorial legacy of roses. Her dedication inspired French rose breeders, who took up the cause and dominated the market well into the twentieth century.

Centuries of rose cultivation have produced an astonishing number of varieties, many of which are immensely satisfying to grow in Alberta. The genus Rosa now contains over 150 species with the number growing annually as hybridizers further their art to bring us more hardy shrub roses, hybrid teas, polyanthas, floribundas, grandifloras, miniatures, standard tree roses, ramblers and climbing roses.

DESIGNING WITH SHRUB ROSES

The recent revival of interest in shrub (or hardy) roses reflects a change in attitude toward the use of roses in contemporary gardens. Until recently, the name *rose* was synonymous with fancy tender hybrids. These aristocratic cousins still delight avid gardeners, but the interest in prolific, flowering and disease-resistant shrub rose varieties has spurred rose breeders to develop hardier varieties for Alberta gardeners.

Although the term *shrub rose* refers to a catch-all category, which includes old-fashioned and modern roses and the full and vigorous appearance of wild roses, it is most often associated with hardy species. I use the term *hardy shrub rose* to refer to roses suitable for Alberta gardens. These, depending on location, require little or no winter protection.

Like other modern roses, hardy shrub roses are the result of hybridizing. For example, *Rosa rugosa* 'Theresa Bugnet,' a staple of Alberta gardens since 1950, is the result of a cross between our native wild rose (*Rosa acicularis*) and several others imported from the Soviet Union. The progeny of this particular cross have given us a very hardy and fragrant pink rose.

In formal and informal gardens alike, hardy shrub roses have many virtues. The range of colours, from white through pink to the occasional red, makes them ideal for a variety of garden palettes. The low-growing shrub roses can provide interest in front of informal shrub beds and foundation plantings. The very tall varieties lend delicate pastel colours to arbors or pergolas.

For Alberta gardeners, winter-hardy shrub roses from Agriculture Canada include the popular Explorer and Parkland series, both excellent choices for their recurrent flowering and resistance to disease. From the Explorer series comes the cultivar 'Jens Munk,' which blooms prolifically throughout the summer. Its raspberry pink colour makes it ideal for the informal shrub bed or for grouping beside the clear blue spires of delphiniums. White rose fanciers will take pleasure in the richly fragrant 'Henry Hudson,' another Explorer cultivar. Its pink-tipped buds open to a snow-white display of petals. This versatile rose is an ideal companion to fiery hot pink- and magenta-coloured perennials, where it serves to intensify their colours. If height is desired, consider the Explorers 'John Cabot' and 'Henry Kelsey.' Although officially considered tall shrub roses, they can give the appearance of climbing roses when planted beside trellises or arbors. The cultivar 'John Cabot' bears orchid pink blooms while 'Henry Kelsey' produces prolific red flowers with a spicy fragrance. Other tall vigorous shrub roses from the Explorer series include the light pink 'John Davis,' the bright pink 'William Baffin,' the soft pink 'Martin Frobisher' and the crimson pink 'David Thompson.' See your local garden centre for others.

With coppery red petals surrounding bright yellow centres, these showy shrub roses make excellent companions for yellow hybrid lilies or clear blue delphiniums.

From the Parkland series, you may enjoy the upright 'Morden Blush,' which provides a variety of colour, depending on temperature. In cold temperatures the blooms are light pink, while in hot temperatures they range from ivory to white. Another Parkland favourite is the 'Morden Ruby,' whose red blooms create a striking contrast to white companion plantings of Asiatic lilies or a floral carpet of snow-in-summer (*Cerastium tomentosum*). Equally at home in shrub beds or flower gardens, the 'Morden Ruby' produces long-lasting double red blooms.

DESIGNING WITH TENDER ROSES

Hybrid teas are perhaps the most widely grown roses in the world. Years of breeding and interbreeding between hybrid perpetuals and tea roses have resulted in these long-stemmed Valentines Day aris-

tocrats. These deliciously scented roses range in colour from white through lavender and pink to warm sassy yellow, orange and red. A dazzling display can be created by devoting an entire flower bed exclusively to hybrid teas. Grouping them will not only help reduce maintenance, but will provide a wonderful intensity of colour and fragrance especially if your rose garden design includes a bench or patio. If garden space is limited, hybrid teas can be grown in containers for your deck or patio. The cultivars 'Chicago Peace,' 'Chrysler Imperial,' 'Garden Party' and 'Golden Jubilee' are excellent choices. However, the bit of paradise that hybrid teas bring to the garden is not yours without some diligence. Generally, hybrid teas are not hardy in Alberta and will require protection to survive our winters—a small price to pay for these tender beauties.

Polyantha roses are the result of crossings between *Rosa multiflora* and other hybrids. Named for the Greek word for *many flowered,* polyanthas produce clusters of smaller flowers, sometimes scented but always exquisite. Blooms are single, double or semi-double, in white, red, yellow, orange and, of course, pastel shades of pink. The cultivars 'China Doll,' 'Snow White' and 'Sparkler' are perfect choices for Alberta gardens. Polyanthas are best know for their progeny, the floribunda roses.

Floribunda roses exhibit the best qualities of their *Rosa multiflora* and hybrid parents. From the hybrid teas come the delicately shaped blossoms and from the polyanthas come the improved vigour. Floribundas bear clusters of blooms on stems of medium height. Many cultivars are available in colours to suit virtually any taste. The orange 'Fire King,' white 'Evening Star' and yellow 'Little Darling' are delightful.

Grandiflora roses, in turn, are the result of crosses

between hybrid teas and floribundas. The combination of increased hardiness and continual bloom from the floribundas and the flower form and long stem from the hybrid teas has made grandifloras a dramatic addition to the rose garden. Borne singly or in small clusters, their blooms make colourful companions to other ornamental shrubs. Consider using the pink-blend 'Pink Parfait,' the orange-blend 'Arizona' or the pink 'Queen Elizabeth' to add a splash of colour next to a dwarf mugo pine (*Pinus mugo* var. *pumilo*) or in front of a cotoneaster hedge (*Cotoneaster lucidus*).

Miniature roses can be enjoyed in even the smallest of gardens. Tiny perfectly formed blooms are borne on plants about 30 cm (12") tall, making them ideal for edging flower or shrub beds. As container plants, their dainty flowers can be enjoyed on patios, decks and balconies. The pink 'Cupcake,' red 'Dreamglo' and mauve 'Lavender Jewel' are especially beautiful.

With a little diligence, every Alberta gardener can enjoy deliciously scented hybrid teas. Plant in a wind-sheltered location receiving at least six hours of sunlight per day.

Standard tree roses are primarily hybrid teas, floribundas or grandifloras grafted onto tall brier stalks. These aristocratic tree roses can add charm and interest to your garden, especially as accent plants. Imagine a doorway graced by two terra cotta pots containing scented pastel tree roses underplanted with cascading lobelia (*Lobelia erinus*) and trailing ivies (*Hedera* spp.). Or consider using a standard tree rose as the featured plant in a rose garden with lower-growing floribundas and grandifloras radiating from it. Take note, however, that specialized procedures are necessary to overwinter standards.

Climbing and rambler roses rarely fail to capture the hearts of rose fanciers when their scented blooms are seen cascading over trelliswork and arbors. Because most flowers are produced on two-year wood, annual dieback sometimes limits the flowering of these tender roses. However, the red 'Blaze' or pink 'Morning Jewel' are worthy of trial.

SELECTING A SITE

For optimum growth, plant roses in well-drained, fertile loamy soil. The addition of well-rotted manure, compost or peat moss will improve most soil conditions. Most roses prefer slightly acidic soil with a pH between 5.5 and 6.5. If you are unsure of the pH quality of your soil, have a soil test done and get expert advice on making necessary amendments.

When planning your rose plantings, choose a site that receives adequate sunlight, drainage and air circulation. All roses require six hours of direct sunlight per day to thrive, but plan to provide for some afternoon shade to help keep the blossom colours from fading. Bear in mind that roses aren't good competitors and shouldn't be planted too close to large trees. Since roses require adequate drainage, avoid planting them in low spots where water pools after a rain. Good air movement goes a long way toward reducing foliage diseases, but take care to offer your roses' delicate blooms some protection from damaging winds.

PLANTING INSTRUCTIONS

Roses can be purchased as bare-root plants or as potted plants. Bare-root plants, typically ordered from a catalogue, should arrive between late April and early May. The new plants should have at least three new canes. Plant them, using the following guidelines, on a cloudy spring afternoon to reduce transplant shock.

1. Soak the roots in water overnight or at least for a few hours, as roots often dry out during shipment.

2. Before planting, become familiar with the mature size of your roses and space accordingly. Dig a hole 45–50 cm (18–20") deep and wide to allow for unrestricted root growth.

3. Fill the hole about 1/3 full with amended soil: equal parts of peat moss, perlite or vermiculite and garden loam. Shape the soil into a cone in the bottom of the hole.

4. Remove the plants from the water and prune off any broken or ragged roots.

5. Place roots over the mound so that they fan out with no restrictions.

6. Fill the hole 3/4 full, gently tamping the soil to anchor the roots firmly. The graft union should be at least 10 cm (4") below the soil line. (A recent trend is to plant long-rooted plants on a slant instead of upright to increase the amount of winter protection.)

With their delicate colours and shapes, it's little wonder that long-stemmed hybrid tea roses have become the aristocrats of Valentines Day.

7. Flood the hole with water to remove air pockets. Once the water has been absorbed into the soil, completely fill the hole with soil.

8. After covering the roots with soil, heap perlite or vermiculite over the graft union to assist new shoots in pushing up through the soil. (Although recommended by some growers, this step is not always necessary.)

9. Create a saucerlike depression around the plant for efficient water use.

10. Water thoroughly, then cover with burlap or mound peat moss or loose garden soil to the tips of the canes to protect the plant from cold temperatures and drying winds. Keep the soil moist and leave the

protection in place until growth has started. If soil has been mounded over the graft union, remove it slowly over a period of two weeks.

11. After about six weeks a water-soluble fertilizer can be applied. Follow manufacturer's directions.

12. Label the rose cultivar correctly.

Potted roses, on the other hand, can be planted throughout the growing season as long as the danger of spring frost has passed. Both tender and shrub roses are available in pots at garden centres in pots. These should be planted after the last spring frost at the same soil height as they were in the container. The graft bud union should be 10–15 cm (4–6") below the soil line. If the roses already have leaves and blooms, it is not necessary to mound soil to the tips of the canes.

CARING FOR ROSES
Watering

A constant moisture supply is critical to establishing new roses. Give them the equivalent of at least 2.5–4 cm (1–1.5") of rain per week. Apply the water directly to the soil as wet foliage is susceptible to diseases.

Fertilizing and Mulching

Applying well-rotted manure or compost to rose beds in spring provides the nutrients necessary for optimum growth and the mulch needed for moisture retention and soil temperature reduction on hot summer days. A supplemental application of an all-purpose fertilizer may be necessary. Follow manufacturers' instructions. Be sure to keep all fertilizers and manure a few inches away from the canes. Avoid fertilizing after mid-August to discourage new growth.

Controlling Pests and Diseases

Roses sometimes fall victim to insects and diseases. The best defense against such invasions is providing optimum growing conditions—strong healthy plants are better equipped to withstand pests. Part of your garden routine should include regular inspection of your roses for signs of plant stress. Common symptoms include swollen stems (called *galls*), discoloured leaves, spotty leaves or buds with holes, buds that fail to open and fine webs on the undersides of foliage. At the first sign of a problem, consult your local gardening centre for the best remedy.

CARING FOR TENDER ROSES IN WINTER

In Alberta, tender roses such as hybrid teas, floribundas, grandifloras, miniatures and standard tree roses require winter protection. If left to face the winter elements without it, roses will succumb to the repeated freezing and thawing common to much of the province throughout the winter months. In the late autumn give your roses a good soaking along with all your perennials and trees. Prune tender roses (except standards) to a height of 25–30 cm (10–12") and destroy the cut branches. Cover the graft union and the lower branches with peat moss or sawdust or a combination of both. If wind is a problem, cover your roses with evergreen boughs or burlap.

To overwinter standard roses completely bury them on their sides in the garden or bring them into a cool dark room (5–7°C / 41–45°F). If you choose to overwinter your standards out of doors, bury them after the first killing frost has wilted the foliage. Simply bend the canes over and lay them gently on the ground. Weight them down with evergreen boughs and bury them under 60 cm (2') of soil. Uncover them in the spring after the risk of heavy frost has passed (about the time trees burst into leaf). For many dedicated rose gardeners, a solarium or greenhouse is an ideal location for overwintering standard roses. If you choose to overwinter your standard roses indoors, keep the soil lightly moist for the duration of the dormant period.

Before purchasing roses, visit your local nursery or garden centre to discover which varieties do well in your specific area. Also consider joining your local rose society, which can provide valuable cultural information and planning ideas. In spite of rumours to the contrary, roses are not difficult to grow in Alberta if gardeners invest the appropriate time and energy in thoughtful planning and diligent care. What queen ever deserved less?

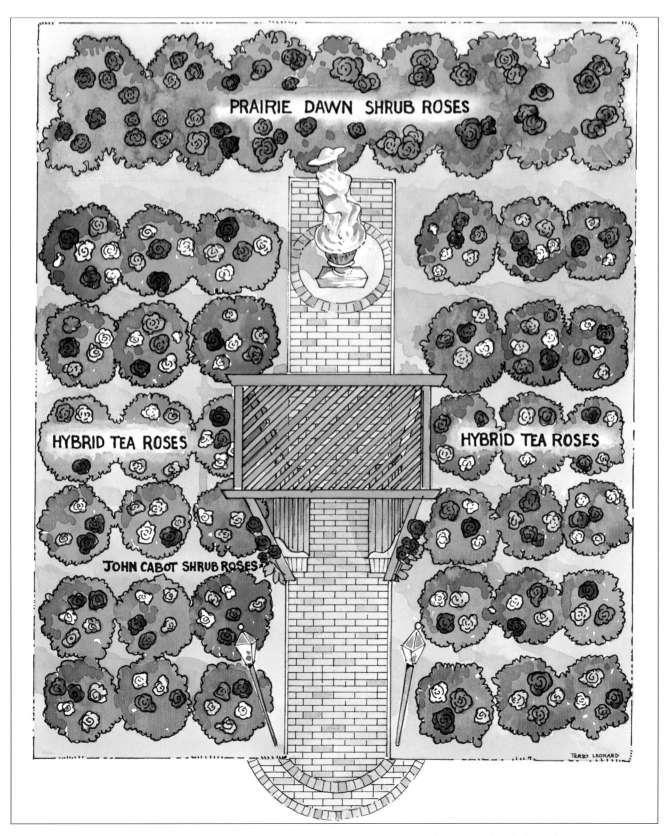

This highly formal garden relies on symmetrical balance to showcase a profusion of colours and scents. The arbor extends an invitation for quiet contemplation.

THE ROSE GARDEN

COMMON NAME	BOTANICAL NAME	HEIGHT	SPREAD
Shrub Roses			
Wild Rose	*Rosa* acicularis	1 M (3')	1 M (3')
Charles Albanel	*Rosa* x 'Charles Albanel'	50 cm (20")	1 M (3')
Cuthbert Grant	*Rosa* x 'Cuthbert Grant'	80 cm–1 M (2.5–3')	80 cm (2.5')
David Thompson	*Rosa* x 'David Thompson'	1.2 M (4')	1.2 M (4')
Henry Hudson	*Rosa* x 'Henry Hudson'	50–70 cm (1.5–2.3')	1 M (3')
Henry Kelsey	*Rosa* x 'Henry Kelsey'	2–2.5 M (7–8')	2 M (7')
Jens Munk	*Rosa* x 'Jens Munk'	1 M (3')	1 M (3')
John Cabot	*Rosa* x 'John Cabot'	2.5–3 M (8–10')	1.5–2 M (5–7')
John Davis	*Rosa* x 'John Davis'	2–2.5 M (7–8')	1–1.5 M (3–5')
Martin Frobisher	*Rosa* x 'Martin Frobisher'	1.5–2 M (5–7')	1.5–2 M (3–5')
Morden Blush	*Rosa* x 'Morden Blush'	50 cm–1 M (1.5–3')	50 cm–1 M (1.5–3')
Morden Ruby	*Rosa* x 'Morden Ruby'	1 M (3')	1 M (3')
Prairie Joy	*Rosa* x 'Prairie Joy'	1–1.5 M (3–5')	1–1.5 M (3–5')
Theresa Bugnet	*Rosa* x 'Theresa Bugnet'	2 M (7')	1.5 M (5')
William Baffin	*Rosa* x 'William Baffin'	2.5–3 M (8–10')	2 M (7')
Hybrid Teas			
Chicago Peace	*Rosa* x 'Chicago Peace'	50 cm–1 M (1.5–3')	varies
Chrysler Imperial	*Rosa* x 'Chrysler Imperial'	50–80 cm (1.5–2.5')	varies
Garden Party	*Rosa* x 'Garden Party'	50–80 cm (1.5–2.5')	varies
Golden Jubilee	*Rosa* x 'Golden Jubilee'	50–80 cm (1.5–2.5')	varies
Peace	*Rosa* x 'Peace'	50 cm–1M (1.5–3')	varies
Polyanthas			
China Doll	*Rosa* x 'China Doll'	30–50 cm (12–20")	varies
Snow White	*Rosa* x 'Snow White'	30–50 cm (12–20")	varies
Sparkler	*Rosa* x 'Sparkler'	30–50 cm (12–20")	varies
The Fairy	*Rosa* x 'The Fairy'	40–60 cm (16–24")	varies
Floribundas			
Evening Star	*Rosa* x 'Evening Star'	50 cm–1 M (1.5–3')	varies
Fire King	*Rosa* x 'Fire King'	50 cm–1 M (1.5–3')	varies
Little Darling	*Rosa* x 'Little Darling'	50–80 cm (1.5–2.5')	varies
Grandifloras			
Arizona	*Rosa* x 'Arizona'	40–90 cm (16–36")	varies
Pink Parfait	*Rosa* x 'Pink Parfait'	40–90 cm (16–36")	varies
Queen Elizabeth	*Rosa* x 'Queen Elizabeth'	50 cm–1 M (1.5–3')	varies
Miniatures			
Cupcake	*Rosa* x 'Cupcake'	30–60 cm (12–24")	varies
Dreamglo	*Rosa* x 'Dreamglo'	30–60 cm (12–24")	varies
Judy Fischer	*Rosa* x 'Judy Fischer'	30–60 cm (12–24")	varies
Lavender Jewel	*Rosa* x 'Lavender Jewel'	30–60 cm (12–24")	varies
Starina	*Rosa* x 'Starina'	30–60 cm (12–24")	varies
Climbing and Ramblers			
Blaze	*Rosa* x 'Blaze'	1–2 M (3–7')	varies
Morning Jewel	*Rosa* x 'Morning Jewel'	1–2 M (3–7')	varies

FOLIAGE COLOUR	FLOWER COLOUR	COMMENTS
green	pink	suitable for naturalizing
green	red	scented
green	red	strongly scented, semi-double blooms
green	pink to red	scented, repeat bloomer
green	white	apple-scented blooms, repeat bloomer
green	red	scented, repeat bloomer
green	pink	prolific bloomer, extended blooming period
green	pink	strong arching canes
green	pink	spicy scent, trailing growth habit
green	pink	scented
green	pink to white	prolific blooms, extended bloom period
green	red	repeat bloomer
green	pink	good hedge rose, disease resistant
green	pink	attractive branches in winter
green	pink	strong arching stems, repeat bloomer
green	pink blend	slight scented, large pointed blossoms
green	red	strong scented, abundant blooms
green	white	nice accent, repeat bloomer
green	yellow blend	scented, repeat bloomer
green	yellow blend	scented, large pointed blooms
green	pink	ideal in containers, repeat bloomer
green	white	repeat bloomer
green	red	repeat bloomer
green	pink	showy, repeat bloomer
green	white	repeat bloomer
green	orange	repeat bloomer
green	yellow	scented, repeat bloomer
green	orange blend	strongly scented
green	pink blend	large cup-shaped blooms
green	pink	large pointed blooms, repeat bloomer
green	pink	cup-shaped blooms, repeat bloomer
green	red blend	pointed blooms, repeat bloomer
green	pink	repeat bloomer
green	mauve	repeat bloomer
green	orange	repeat bloomer
green	red	cup-shaped blooms, repeat bloomer
green	pink	cup-shaped blooms, repeat bloomer

THE WATER GARDEN

"Starry river-buds glimmered by,
And round them the soft stream
did glide and dance
With a motion of sweet sound
and radiance"
–Percy Bysshe Shelley

Water is a magical element in gardens, filling them with the soothing music of nature and reflecting the changing hues of skies. By a strange wizardry, water's life-giving qualities influence the moods of entire gardens. In a quiet reflecting pool—with colourful floating water lilies and edged by marsh marigolds, flowering rush and irises—water evokes peace and contemplation. In fountains or waterfalls, water becomes a source of sound and energy, which filters out unwanted noise and has a mesmerizing attraction on watchers and listeners. With such a range of expression, it's easy to see why water gardens are becoming one of the fastest growing trends in garden design.

The exquisite snow-white blooms of hydrangeas add elegance to this water garden's display.

If you have a balanced water ecosystem, pumps and filters are unnecessary. However, if your plan includes cascading or moving water, you will require a pump to provide lift. The size of pump is determined by the volume of water and the height of the lift. Check local garden, pet and hardware centres for the correct pump specifications.

❦

Bring your water garden alive by night with subtle indirect lighting or the gentle effect of candles or torches. Consult a qualified electrician before attempting any electrical installations.

DESIGNING WITH WATER

Because it will fill any shape, water is equally at home in formal and informal settings, but because it tends to dominate garden compositions, you should be careful to design displays to suit the scale and character of your garden. Traditional fountains or geometric reflecting pools may be better suited to formal gardens, while cascading waterfalls are better in informal settings. Small ornamental containers filled with water can add gentle surprises to small alcoves in just about any setting.

The best aquatic gardens are usually an integral part of existing gardens. Like shrub beds and flower borders, they offer subtle rhythms of seasonal colour, form and texture. A balanced distribution of these design elements will not only arouse botanical interest but will provide a sense of structure to the overall design.

SELECTING A CONTAINER

Almost any container can become a water garden—from a discarded bathtub or old canner to a preformed fiberglass shell or concrete or PVC (polyvinyl chloride) liner. Water gardens can be as simple and inexpensive as a half barrel of water with a single splendid lily and a couple of goldfish or as complex and pricey as formal fountains or naturally styled waterfalls replete with bridges and statuary.

Concrete-lined ponds, depending on the size and site, are expensive and laborious to install and must be reinforced at the top of the pool to protect against the great pressure exerted by freezing. Better choices for Alberta gardeners are fiberglass shells or PVC liners, which are affordable, relatively easy to install and more durable in our climate. PVC liners have the added advantages of being nontoxic and possessing ultraviolet inhibitors.

SELECTING A SITE

The site of your water garden depends on your overall plan. If you prefer blooming water plants, locate your pool in full sunlight to provide the warm water and the six to eight hours of sunlight per day that water lilies need to flourish. If you must choose a shady location, take care not to place the garden directly under trees where roots will interfere with digging and falling leaves will pollute the water.

When choosing the size and shape of your pond, take cues from the surrounding environment. A rectangular pond will suit a more formal design.

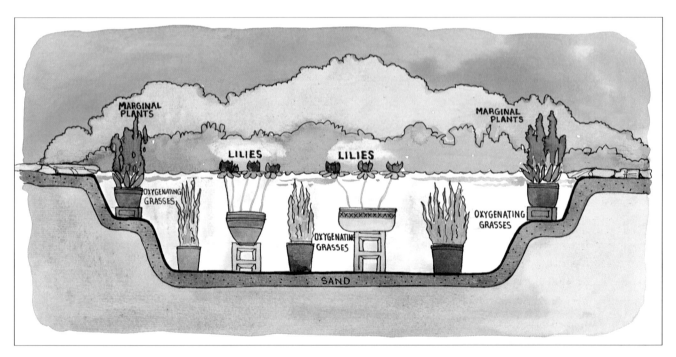

This cross-section of a water garden illustrates construction details as well as the planting arrangement of marginal plants and oxygenating grasses and lilies.

A kidney-shaped or other free-form pond, on the other hand, complements an informal garden. Be sure to locate your pond where you can enjoy it from your favourite vantages, such as a patio, deck or other garden structure.

CREATING A LARGE WATER GARDEN

1. Mark out free-form ponds with a length of garden hose to help you visualize the final design of the pond. Use stakes and garden twine to mark out rectangular designs. To lay out a perfectly rectangular or square pool, use the carpenter's triangle rule. Starting from the stake at your first corner, mark the 91.5-cm (3') point in one direction and the 122-cm (4') point in the other. When the diagonal measurement between the points is 152.5 cm (5'), you have a 90° angle. Measure and stake the two corners extending from your carpenter's triangle and then measure to your fourth corner. To double-check that all four corners are square, measure diagonally from corner to corner. These measurements must be equal.

2. Dig the hole for the water garden to the desired shape and size, making sure the depth is at least 46 cm (18"). Depth is a critical factor of your pond's suc-cess. If it is shallower, the water temperature will change too easily and the ecological balance will be harder to maintain. Allow for a 5–10 cm (2–4") layer of sand beneath the liner. Use a carpenter's level to ensure the bottom is horizontal. If you desire varying levels in the pond, dig in tiers at near-90° angles to prevent the liner from sagging. About 20–30 cm (8–12") below the top of the excavation, create a 30 cm- (12") wide ledge around the perimeter. This ledge will be ideal for growing a variety of attractive marginal plants.

3. Smooth out the sand with a broom to get an even surface. Remove any protruding rocks or sharp objects that could damage the liner.

4. To calculate the size of liner you need, add twice the pond's depth to both its width and length. For example, if your pond is 122 cm (4') wide by 183 cm (6') long and 61 cm (2') deep, the size of your lining is calculated as follows:

> Width: 2 x 61 cm + 122 cm = 2.5 M (2 x 2' + 4' = 8')
> Length: 2 x 61 cm + 183 cm = 3 M (2 x 2' + 6' = 10')
> Allow for an extra 30 cm (12") of liner all the way around the excavation.

5. Place the properly sized liner in position, making sure it isn't under tension. A warm sunny day is ideal

for this task as the liner's flexibility is increased. Secure the liner with bricks or rocks.

6. Fill the pond with water and let it stand for 24–48 hours to allow the liner to settle and the chlorinating agents to disperse. If you are unsure of the quality of your tap water, have it examined by an independent laboratory. Generally speaking, most urban tap water is of suitable quality for pond life.

7. Fold under the edges of the liner and place good-sized flat rocks, bricks or paving stones, depending on your design preference, around the perimeter to conceal the fold. To create a natural look, place the rocks slightly overhanging the edge of the pond. Smaller rocks or gravel can be used to fill in the spaces between the larger pieces.

CREATING A MINIATURE WATER GARDEN

A half barrel makes a fascinating miniature water habitat in confined spaces. Be sure to line the barrel with plastic or PVC to protect plants from toxins that may be present in the wood. Then cover the bottom with 5–8 cm (2–3") of a sand and gravel mixture. Place a few small rocks on the top to provide shelter for small aquatic wildlife. Then fill the barrel with fresh water. If you use tap water, wait at least 24 hours so the chlorine can dissipate before you introduce your plants.

SELECTING WATER PLANTS

Water plants excite and enliven a garden. Some water garden enthusiasts are content with a couple of

If your space is limited, try containers, which can support stunning displays of exotic star-shaped blooms. They will add refreshing ambiance to any deck or patio.

Siberian irises bear a profusion of delicate flowers atop gracefully arching foliage. Perfect accent plants for bordering ponds.

Suggested Pond Formula for Water Garden Plants and Animal Life:
For every 1 square metre (1 square yard) of pond surface area, include 2 bunches of oxygenating plants, 1 medium to large water lily, 12 water snails and 2 small fish.

exotic water lilies floating on the surface of a small tranquil pond. Others prefer a more elaborate tangle of lush green foliage that includes an assortment of gracefully arching strap- and heart-shaped leaves. To strengthen the visual impact of your design, plant in odd-numbered groups of three, five or seven, keeping in mind the proportion of the plant size to its surroundings. For example, the small urban water garden may require a planting of only a few flowering rushes (*Butomus umbellatus*) for a vertical accent. Conversely, a large pond on an acreage may need a vertical accent of more than twenty irises to achieve the same fullness of effect. Other water garden plants, like the decorative Siberian iris (*Iris sibirica*), are most appealing in mass groupings. Planted in casual drifts, these stunning perennials appear natural and fluid. Whatever water plants you choose—from jewel-toned primroses (*Primula* spp.) and statuesque yellow flag irises (*Iris pseudocorus*) to spectacular water lilies (*Nymphaea* spp.)—there are colours, textures and forms to suit any purpose.

Water plants are necessary for an ecologically balanced pond. Besides their decorative contribution, they provide oxygen for fish and screen out some direct sunlight, reducing the growth of algae. Water plants suitable for Alberta gardens are available in several types, some of which are typically purchased in pots. These can be simply placed in the water garden at their recommended depths. (Many growers supply planting information with your purchase, and these special instructions should be noted.)

Water Lilies

With their dazzling colours and sweet perfumes, water lilies (*Nymphaea* spp.) are the stars of the water garden. Interestingly, the ancient Egyptians associated them with eternal life—possibly because the flowers of some species withdraw under the water at sunset and reemerge with the first warm rays of the morning sun. Water lilies are ideal for adding bright splashes of colour to a pond or for a single flower display in a half barrel or water-tight crock. Lilies are available in a wide variety of colours to suit any planting scheme. Some bloom in the daytime, while others open at night, extending the enjoyment of the water garden into the evening.

In large ponds, consider the cultivar 'Attraction,' which has large garnet-red blooms with white tips. And don't overlook the fragrant double-pink blooms of 'Hollandia' or the large star-shaped flowers of 'Rose Arey.' In small ponds or tubs, the cultivar 'James Brydon' bears miniature rosy red blooms and releases a delicious applelike fragrance. Other cultivars bearing miniature blooms include 'Marliacea Albida' and 'Pygmaea Alba,' both of which feature white flowers, and the cultivar 'Pygmaea Helvola,' which bears canary yellow

Plant enchanting shooting stars en masse near the water garden. They look particularly stunning next to dark blue viola.

Water lilies are the stars of the water garden. These beauties are available in an exotic range of colours and fragrances.

blooms. If your water garden is illuminated, you may be tempted by the night-blooming cultivar 'Sir Galahad' with its large white blooms sitting prominently above shiny scallop-edged foliage.

Planting Water Lilies

Water lilies should be planted in a sunny area of the pond away from the turbulence created by a fountain or waterfall.

1. Fill a container two-thirds full of heavy loam or clay and hollow out a planting hole for the lily. (Organic matter such as grass, leaves and peat should not be used as they will foul the water.)

2. Place the lily rhizome in the hole with its crown just above soil level, and holding it in position, gently add soil around the crown.

3. Cover the soil with a 1.25-cm (.5") layer of sand or fine gravel. Firm the soil and water the plant thoroughly to remove air pockets.

4. Sink the pot into the pond so that the rim is 15–30 cm (6–12") below the surface. As water lilies grow they should be lowered to at least 30 cm (12") but can be sunk as deep as 152 cm (5'). If installing water lilies in a deeper pool, raise the containers on bricks. As the leaf stems extend, the bricks can be removed.

Floating Plants

Floating aquatics, which feed through roots suspended in the water, add an exotic dimension to the water garden. The water hyacinth (*Eichhornia crassipes*) with its lavender-blue orchidlike flowers is an ideal choice for Alberta water gardens. It adds not only colour but is instrumental in maintaining water quality by providing shade, absorbing excess nutrients, helping to control algae and purifying the water. To add texture, consider water lettuce (*Pistia stratiotes*) with its wrinkled light green leaves. It will tolerate some shade but needs a lot of growing space so use it sparingly. Like the water hyacinth, it is beneficial to the pond's environment.

Submerged and Emergent Plants

These decorative aquatic plants produce essential oxygen for pond organisms while helping to control excessive algae growth. Like water lilies, they are planted in containers of heavy soil and placed at appropriate depths.

Arrowhead (*Sagittaria* spp.), with its flowers borne on spikelets, is an attractive addition to the edges of the pond. A shallow water plant, it should be placed so that its pot is just below the water's surface. In warm water the arrowhead can double its height. Another delightful addition to the shallow water region of your garden is the water violet (*Hottonia palustris*), which thrives in calm clean water. Its lilac-coloured yellow-throated flowers are held above the water. The leaves are very finely cut. For deeper water plants, consider the brilliant yellows of water fringe (*Nymphoides peltata*) and yellow pond lily (*Nuphar variegatum*). Water fringe, with its small heart-shaped leaves, resembles a tiny water lily and is ideal for miniature gardens. The blooms of the yellow pond lily are borne above the water on long buoyant stalks. Because they are native aquatics they may be too vigorous for a small pond but will be perfect in large natural water gardens.

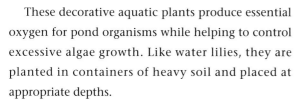
Tucked between lichen and moss-covered boulders, primroses cast a golden glow with their jewel-toned colours.

Bog and Marginal Plants

Making the transition between the pond and the rest of the garden are plants that grow alongside the pool in moist soil or with their roots submerged.

Among the best choices for waterside plantings are the Siberian iris (*Iris sibirica*), yellow flag iris (*Iris pseudocorus*) and marsh marigold (*Caltha palustris*). The Siberian is a hardy perennial with flower colours ranging from pale blue to purple. The vigorous sun-loving yellow flag iris, with its charming yellow flowers and swordlike leaves, is ideal for providing late spring colour. Like the yellow flag iris, the marsh marigold is most at home in full sunlight. A native to the wetlands of Canada, it has yellow cup-shaped flowers with heart-shaped leaves.

For moist shady locations bordering water gardens, consider primroses (*Primula* spp.), but avoid planting these spring beauties directly in standing water. When planted *en masse,* their delicate flowers provide bright splashes of spring colour. Many species and cultivars are available.

Among the best choices for shallow water plantings are water arum, flowering rush and water hawthorn. Water arum (*Calla palustris*) is a familiar plant that makes its home in shallow ponds and boggy places in Alberta. The large flowerlike spathe encloses a tiny flower. Orange-red berries may appear. Flowering rush (*Butomus umbellatus*) sports showy large umbels of pink flowers and purple leaves, making it an attractive addition to the water garden. Water hawthorn (*Aponogeton distachyus*) has strap-shaped deep green leaves and white vanilla-scented flowers with black centres. Most showy in the cool water of spring and late autumn, it disappears in the warm water that comes with summer.

Bright yellow coreopsis complement the mauve-pink umbels of flowering rushes in this informal water planting.

Oxygenating Plants

Oxygenating plants absorb carbon dioxide and release beneficial oxygen and carbohydrates into the water. Because they compete for the same food and light as algae, they keep the water cleaner. They also provide egg-laying sites, food and hiding places for the fish. The seaweedlike elodea (*Elodea canadensis*) is an ideal addition to Alberta water gardens.

AQUATIC ANIMAL LIFE

Water gardens, by their very nature, extend an invitation to a variety of animal life. Damselflies, dragonflies and birds will be attracted to the water for both recreation and lunch. And resident frogs and insects will bring the soothing sounds of nature to the garden.

PREPARING FOR WINTER

Overwintering techniques will vary depending upon pond size and plant species. Water lilies—excluding the hardy yellow pond lily (*Nuphar variegatum*)—should be taken from the pool, kept in a closed plastic garbage bag and stored in a cool dark area. Floating and oxygenating plants can be overwintered in a tropical fish tank. Siberian iris, marsh marigold and other bog and marginal plants are generally hardy and can be left in the ground. If the pond is relatively small, it should be drained and cleaned.

THE WATER GARDEN

COMMON NAME	BOTANICAL NAME	FLOWER COLOUR
Water Hawthorn	*Aponogeton distachyus*	white
Flowering Rush	*Butomus umbellatus*	pink
Water Arum	*Calla palustris*	inconspicuous
Marsh Marigold	*Caltha palustris*	yellow
Shooting Star	*Dodeocatheon media*	pink, rose
Water Hyacinth	*Eichhornia crassipes*	violet
Elodea	*Elodea canadensis*	inconspicuous
Water Violet	*Hottonia palustris*	lilac with yellow throat
Yellow Flag Iris	*Iris pseudocorus*	yellow
Siberian Iris	*Iris sibirica*	blue to white
Yellow Pond Lily	*Nuphar variegatum*	yellow
European Water Lily	*Nymphaea alba* var. *rubra*	rose
Water Lily	*Nymphaea* 'Attraction'	red
Water Lily	*Nymphaea* 'Hollandia'	pink
Water Lily	*Nymphaea* 'James Brydon'	red
Water Lily	*Nymphaea* 'Rose Arey'	pink
Water Lily	*Nymphaea* 'Sir Galahad'	white
Pygmy Water Lily	*Nymphaea tetregona*	white
Pygmaea Helvola Water Lily	*Nymphaea* x *helvola* 'Pygmaea Helvola'	yellow
Marliacea Albida Water Lily	*Nymphaea* x *marliacea* var. *albida*	pink-white
Water Fringe	*Nymphoides peltata*	yellow
Water Lettuce	*Pistia stratiotes*	inconspicuous
Primrose	*Primula* spp.	wide variety
Arrowhead	*Sagittaria* spp.	white

93

FOLIAGE FORM	FOLIAGE COLOUR	COMMENTS
straplike	green	unusual arrangement of floating leaves
strap-shaped	green	unusual vertical accent
oval to heart-shaped	green	attractive marginal plant
heart-shaped	shiny green	early spring colour
	green	
unusual shape	green	floating plant, tolerates partial shade
seaweedlike	green	vigorous oxygenator
feathery	green	attractive water plant
sword-shaped	green	hardy, good colour
sword-shaped	green	hardy, good colour
flat, circular	green	aggressive in small ponds
flat, circular	green	robust
flat, circular	green	suitable for large ponds
flat, circular	green	fragrant blooms
flat, circular	green	cup-shaped blooms with yellow centres
flat, circular	green	delicately scented blooms
flat with scalloped edges	green	evening flowering
flat, circular	mottled	hardy, parent of many hybrids
flat, circular	green	dwarf, suitable for containers
flat, circular	green	scented, bright yellow stamens
circular	mottled	fast spreading
lettucelike	blue green	floating plant, attractive foliage
varies	green	early colour, avoid standing water
arrowlike	green	attractive en masse

CHAPTER

9

THE SCENTED GARDEN

*"Smell is a potent wizard that
transports us across thousands of miles
and all the years we have lived"*

–Helen Keller

The fragrance of lilacs or the ambrosia of certain roses is wonderfully evocative and capable of stirring in us the most long-forgotten memories. Nothing soothes and refreshes the spirit like the smells of moist earth, pine needles and especially perfumed flowers. Design your outdoor living space to include fragrant plants, and its beauty will extend to the nose as well as the eye. And as an added benefit, scent will extend an invitation to the great pollinators of the world, the bees, butterflies and other conveyors of pollen.

Scented flowers, especially the venerable rose, have a long history of association with love and passion. When Cleopatra welcomed Mark Antony to her chambers, it was covered more than a foot deep in aromatic petals. Cleopatra knew how to please her guests, for few cultures have been as obsessed by the power of floral fragrances as the Romans. As a matter of course, roses were strewn at ceremonies and public gatherings. The Emperor Nero spent extraordinary sums on roses for his banquets, even showering his guests with so many petals that one man was reported to have smothered to death under their intoxicating weight.

Until very recently, modern plant breeders tended to value qualities such as colour and size over scent. But now, with our renewed desire for natural fragrances, the scented garden has made a triumphant return.

Scents or perfumes are the essential oils found in the flowers or leaves of plants. In flowers, these take the form of complex mixtures of chemical compounds that give a particular variety a distinct fragrance. The lovely Damask rose, for example, supplies attar of roses, an essential oil that found its way into the perfumer's

Bordering a sunny flower bed or next to a pathway, sweet-scented annual alyssum will delight visitors with mats of perfumed flowers.

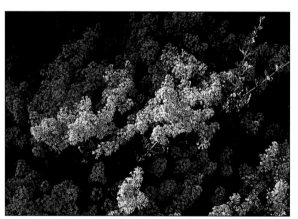

A fresh bouquet of lilacs is wonderfully evocative. Enjoy these fragrant shrubs near a sunny patio or window.

repertoire as early as the time of the Pharaohs. Perfumed leaves are less chemically complex than flowers. Best known for offering scented foliage are culinary and medicinal herbs. Parsley, sage, rosemary and thyme are lyrics from a ballad as well as perfumers in the garden.

SELECTING A SITE

Wise gardeners plant scented flowers or trees in sunny sheltered locations where fragrance can best be appreciated. Tuck a garden bench beside the perfumed branches of an ornamental flowering crabapple tree. Bring fragrance to the deck or patio with scented borders or containers. Position scented plants near doors or walkways where passersby can lightly crush the leaves to release their fragrant oils. Place scented shrubs beside a window so the early summer breeze can waft their sweet scents throughout the house.

FRAGRANCE THROUGHOUT THE SEASONS

Since many fragrant plants are seasonal in bloom, it's possible to create an evolving scented garden, one filled with fragrance from early spring to late autumn.

The Spring Scented Garden

Chief among the gifts that spring brings to gardens is the invigorating array of fragrant flowers and plants. Among the first scented flowers to greet you in a sunny spring garden are daffodils (*Narcissus* spp.), crocuses (*Crocus* spp.) and tulips (*Tulipa* spp.). Consider a planting of yellow trumpeted daffodils on a small slope, or a blue carpet of crocuses tucked beside the garden shed or another place where you'll

Hummingbirds are attracted to colourful bee balm, which smells deliciously of citrus and spice. Mauve, red or white flowers are produced atop tall stems.

spend time working in the spring. Tulips are available in a wide variety of heights, colours and forms. Choose from among early, mid- and late-flowering tulips and daffodils to create a succession of fragrance throughout the season.

The flowering crabapple (*Malus* spp.) is a favourite for its delicately perfumed blossoms. With flowers in subtle pastel shades from cotton candy pink to purple-pink to wine red, this attractive ornamental tree is ideal for sunny urban gardens. Wonderfully fragrant lilac shrubs may be planted beside a window so the late spring breeze can carry their sweet scent

indoors. Miniature lilac shrubs are also available. Try the compact cultivar 'Minuet' of the Preston lilacs (*Syringa* x *prestoniae*) for smaller gardens.

In shadier corners of the garden, lily-of-the-valley (*Convallaria majalis*) will produce fragrant nodding white bells held above green straplike leaves. Their delicate appearance and sweet perfume make them an excellent choice for bouquets. The mockorange shrub (*Philadelphus* spp.) will bear fragrant white blooms in profusion in shade. Use it with an underplanting of primrose (*Primula* spp.) to create a carpet of delicate colours and spring perfumes.

The Summer Scented Garden

As the subtle aromas and cheerful blooms of spring fade, the fragrant garden can continue its rhythm with the often more robust and pungent perfumes of summer. In large sunny gardens, peonies (*Paeonia* spp.) can announce the arrival of summer. Their lusciously ruffled plate-sized blooms and heady scent invite close inspection and some cutting shears so they can be enjoyed indoors. You might also consider planting them near a doorway to welcome your guests. Smaller sunny gardens can enjoy the clove-scented blooms of grass pinks (*Dianthus plumarius*). These aromatic perennials are ideal for the rockery or in front of the flower border beside a planting of blue bellflowers (*Campanula* spp.).

Later in the summer garden, the round thistlelike red blossoms of bee balm (*Monarda didyma*) contrast blue skies and love to soak up the summer sun. The flowers and leaves of this perennial are intensely fragrant and have the additional virtue of attracting bees and hummingbirds. It is particularly showy when flirting with blue delphiniums (*Delphinium* spp.).

Extend sunny summer garden pleasures with small pockets of fragrance. Scented perennials such as garden phlox (*Phlox paniculata*) or, if you prefer, annual nicotiana (*Nicotiana* spp.) can be tucked between earlier flowering plants such as peonies (*Paeonia* spp.). Or you might consider planting nicotiana around a sundial so that when visitors pause they are greeted with fragrance.

In partial shade, daylilies (*Hemerocallis* spp.) are one of the most rewarding easy-care perennials. Though not true lilies, they produce lilylike blooms lasting for 24 hours. Careful planning with fragrant varieties will give you a sequence of perfumes throughout the summer. Two deliciously scented cultivars are 'Ginger Whip,' with its ginger-coloured blooms, and 'Heart and Soul,' with its striking blood red blooms.

FRAGRANCE FOR SPECIAL TIMES AND PLACES

The Evening Scented Garden

Many working people cannot retreat to their gardens until the evening, but luckily fragrance in the garden is not reserved to the daylight hours. Besides illuminating the evening garden, white and yellow blooms offer their strongest scents at night. Bring nighttime fragrance to a deck or patio with containers full of evening scented stocks (*Matthiola longipetala*) or sweetly scented nicotiana (*Nicotiana affinis*) and evening primrose (*Oenothera odorata*).

You can add ambiance to an already charming evening scented garden with strings of small lights. One of my gardening friends plants masses of white cascading petunias (*Petunia* x *hybrida*) in a brick planter surrounding her tiny patio. She then attaches small white outdoor lights to the planter's rim. The result is gorgeous.

Scented gardens aren't complete without at least one ruffled and delicately fragrant peony. This long-lived perennial enjoys full sun, well-drained loamy soil and is available in many colours and forms.

Dianthus have an abundance of clove-scented blooms. A terra cotta pot brimming with these colourful annual treasures is perfect for sunny patios.

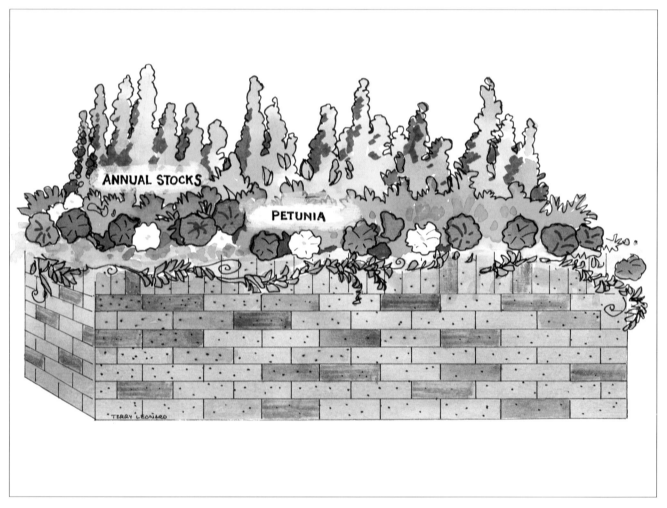

ANNUAL STOCKS

PETUNIA

TERRY LEONARD

The heavily perfumed petunias and annuals stocks in this raised brick planter entice garden guests with their sweet fragrance. As an added attraction, the splashy pink colours harmonize with terra cotta-coloured bricks.

The Scented Container Garden

Containerizing the scented garden has many advantages but chief among them is that containers are moveable, making it easy to place them for greatest effect. Pots of cheerful nasturtiums (*Tropaeolum majus*) with their warm colours and delicious scent will, for example, perfume a well-used terrace for most of the summer. Or you might try heavily perfumed cascading petunias (*Petunia* x *hybrida*). These are available in a wide variety of colours and look especially lovely with sweet alyssum (*Lobularia maritima*) or dianthus (*Dianthus* spp.) as a container companion. Pots of fragrant roses can also be enjoyed on the patio or deck. The compact size of some hybrid teas makes them ideal for containers. Besides offering their sumptuous blooms for viewing, many varieties are sweetly scented. Consider the cultivar 'Alpine Sunset,' which bears fragrant apricot-coloured blooms or the perfumed 'Granada' with red blooms.

Container plantings allow even the smallest of decks and patios to expand vertically. Create a tapestry of perfumed colour with annual sweet peas (*Lathyrus odoratus*) climbing a trellis. Or suspend pots of scented nasturtiums (*Tropaeolum majus*), petunias (*Petunia* x *hybrida*) or geraniums (*Pelargonium graveolens*) overhead, creating a canopy of fragrance. Scented geraniums offer virtually dozens of different scents ranging from roses and lemons to strawberries and even mint chocolate.

THE SCENTED GARDEN

COMMON NAME	BOTANICAL NAME	HEIGHT	SPREAD
Annuals			
Calendula	*Calendula officinalis*	12–60 cm (5–24")	12–30 cm (5–12")
Dianthus	*Dianthus* spp.	15–30 cm (6–12")	15–30 cm (6–12")
Persian Violet	*Exacum affine*	25–30 cm (10–12")	15–20 cm (6–8")
Heliotrope	*Heliotrope arborescens*	45–60 cm (18–24")	30–45 cm (12–18")
Sweet Pea	*Lathyrus odoratus*	15 cm–3 M (6–36")	varies
Dwarf Sweet Pea	*Lathyrus odoratus* 'Knee-Hi'	15–30 cm (6–12")	15 cm (6")
Tall Sweet Pea	*Lathyrus odoratus* 'Spencer Mix'	3 M (10')	5–15 cm (2–6")
Sweet Alyssum	*Lobularia maritima*	5–10 cm (2–4")	25 cm (10")
Stocks	*Matthiola incana*	25–50 cm (10–20")	15–20 cm (6–8")
Evening Scented Stocks	*Matthiola longipetala*	45 cm (18")	10 cm (4")
Four-O'Clocks	*Mirabilis jalapa*	90 cm (36")	90 cm (36")
Lemon Bee Balm	*Monarda citriodora*	45–60 cm (18–24")	30–45 cm (12–18")
Nicotiana	*Nicotiana* spp.	15 cm–1 M (6–36")	varies
Evening Scented Nicotiana	*Nicotiana affinis*	60 cm (24")	varies
Nicotiana	*Nicotiana alata*	15 cm–1 M (6–36")	varies
Evening Primrose	*Oenothera odorata*	15–35 cm (6–14")	15–35 cm (6–14")
Scented Geranium	*Pelargonium graveolens*	varies	varies
Petunia	*Petunia* x *hybrida*	15–30 cm (6–12")	15–30 cm (6–12")
Nasturtium	*Tropaeolum majus*	15–60 cm (6–24")	15–60 cm (6–24")
Perennials			
Rockcress	*Arabis alpina*	15–20 cm (6–8")	30–40 cm (12–16")
Artemisia	*Artemisia* spp.	20–60 cm (8–24")	varies
Lily-of-the-Valley	*Convallaria majalis*	10–20 cm (4–8")	varies
Grass Pinks	*Dianthus plumarius*	40 cm (16")	30 cm (12")
Sweet Woodruff	*Galium odoratum*	30–60 cm (12–24")	30–60 cm (12–24")
Daylily	*Hemerocallis* 'Ginger Whip'	75 cm (30")	varies
Daylily	*Hemerocallis* 'Heart and Soul'	60 cm (24")	varies
Sweet Rocket	*Hesperis matronalis*	1 M (3')	5 cm (2")
Perennial Candytuft	*Iberis sempervirens*	30 cm (12")	30–50 cm (12–20")
Bee Balm	*Monarda didyma*	60–90 cm (24–36")	60 cm (24")
Peony	*Paeonia* spp.	varies	varies
Garden Phlox	*Phlox paniculata*	60–90 cm (24–36")	45–60 cm (18–24")
Primrose	*Primula* spp.	varies	10–30 cm (4–12")
Lavender Cotton	*Santolina chamaecyparissus*	20–45 cm (8–18")	20 cm (8")
Thyme	*Thymus* spp.	varies	varies
Valerian	*Valeriana officinalis*	60–90 cm (24–36")	35–50 cm (14–20")
Bulbs and Others			
Crocus	*Crocus* spp.	10–15 cm (4–6")	varies
Bearded Iris	*Iris* x *germanica*	varies	varies
Asiatic Lily	*Lilium* spp.	1 M (3')	varies
Grape Hyacinth	*Muscari* spp.	10–20 cm (4–8")	varies
Daffodil	*Narcissus* spp.	15–45 cm (6–18")	varies
Tulip	*Tulipa* spp.	5–60 cm (2–24")	varies

FOLIAGE COLOUR	FLOWER COLOUR	COMMENTS
green	orange, yellow	sharp tangy scent, culinary properties
green	red, pink, white	clove-scented blooms
green	lavender	warmth intensifies sweet fragrance
green	purple, violet, white	almond-scented blooms
green	wide variety	honey-scented blooms
green	wide variety	honey-scented blooms
green	wide variety	honey-scented blooms
green	rose, purple, white	sweet fragrance, good for edging paths
green	pink, blue, purple, white	clove-scented blooms
green	purple, white	penetrating clove-scented blooms
green	wide variety	intensified fragrance in evening
green	pinkish white	fragrant foliage when crushed or brushed
green	wide variety	intensified sweet fragrance in evening
green	white	evening-scented blooms
green	wide variety	sweet fragrance
green	yellow, white	orange blossom-scented blooms
varies	wide variety	lemon, clove, apple, mint, rose and chocolate scents
green	wide variety	heavily perfumed blooms
green	orange, yellow	clove- or cinnamon-scented blooms
grey	pink, white	fragrant, suitable for edging paths
silver grey	yellow	sage-scented foliage when crushed
green	white	sweet-scented blooms
green	pink, white	clove-scented blooms
green	yellow	sweet-scented blooms
green	yellow	fragrant blooms
green	red	fragrant blooms
green	mauve pink	honey-scented blooms
green	white	fragrant blooms
green	red, mauve, white	intensely fragrant blooms and leaves
green	wide variety	some cultivars fragrant
green	wide variety	heavily perfumed blooms
green	numerous	some cultivars scented
silver grey	yellow	earth-scented blooms
varies	pink, blue, mauve, white	lemon-, clove- and spice-scented blooms
green	white	fragrant blooms
green	wide variety	delicately scented blooms
green	wide variety	some cultivars with fruity scent
green	wide variety	delicately scented blooms
green	blue, purple, white	masses of fragrant blooms
green	pink, yellow, white orange, cream	some species and cultivars scented
green	wide variety	some species and cultivars lightly scented

COMMON NAME	BOTANICAL NAME	HEIGHT	SPREAD
Scented Shrubs, Trees and Vines			
Ground Clematis	*Clematis recta*	1–1.5 M (3–5')	1–1.5 M (3–5')
Russian Olive	*Eleagnus angustifolia*	4–6 M (13–20')	4–6 M (13–20')
Flowering Crabapple	*Malus* spp.	varies	3–5 M (10–16')
Mockorange	*Philadelphus* spp.	1–2 M (3–7')	1–2 M (3–7')
Minnesota Snowflake Mockorange	*Philadelphus* x *virginalis* 'Minnesota Snowflake'	1–2 M (3–7')	1–2 M (3–7')
Mayday	*Prunus padus* var. *commutata*	12 M (39')	10–12 M (33–39')
Pincherry	*Prunus pennsylvanica*	5 M (16')	3 M (10')
Double Flowering Plum	*Prunus triloba* 'Multiplex'	2–3 M (7–10')	2–3 M (7–10')
Rose	*Rosa* spp.	30 cm–2.5 M (1–8')	60 cm–1.5 M (1–8')
Alpine Sunset Rose	*Rosa* x 'Alpine Sunset'	30–60 cm (1–2')	varies
Granada Rose	*Rosa* x 'Granada'	60–90 cm (2–3')	varies
Meyer Lilac	*Syringa meyeri*	2 M (7')	2 M (7')
Common Lilac	*Syringa vulgaris* 'Charles Joly'	3 M (10')	3 M (10')
Hyacinth Flowered Lilac	*Syringa* x *hyacinthiflora* 'Sister Justina'	3 M (10')	3 M (10')
Preston Lilac	*Syringa* x *prestoniae* 'Isabella'	3 M (10')	3 M (10')
Preston Lilac	*Syringa* x *prestoniae* 'Minuet'	1 M (3')	1–1.5 M (3–5')
Morden Littleleaf Linden	*Tilia cordata* 'Morden'	10–12 M (33–39')	5 M (16')
Dropmore Linden	*Tilia* x *flavescens* 'Dropmore'	10–12 M (33–39')	6 M (20')
Riverbank Grape	*Vitis riparia*	6 M (20')	1 M (3')

FOLIAGE COLOUR	FLOWER COLOUR	COMMENTS
green	white	fragrant blooms
silver	yellow	fragrant blooms
red, green	red, pink, white	fragrant blooms
green	white	some cultivars scented
green	white	strong clove-scented blooms
green	white	fragrant blooms
green	white	cherry-scented blooms
green	pale to deep pink	almond-scented blooms
green	wide variety	variety of fragrances
green	apricot blend	fragrant blooms
green	red blend	fragrant blooms
green	rose purple	fragrant blooms
green	red purple	fragrant blooms
green	white	fragrant blooms
green	rose pink	fragrant blooms
green	purple	fragrant blooms
green	yellow	delicately scented blooms
green	yellow	delicately scented blooms
green	white	fragrant blooms

THE ROCK GARDEN

"When stone is endowed with personality,
one can find it delightful company"

–Chuin Tung

The ancient botanical art of rock gardening descends to us from Zen monks living in the 15th century. It was they, in their quiet search for enlightenment, who first expressed in the gardener's language of design the absolutely beguiling combination of plants and stone—delicate blossoms resting on the strength of stone. Somehow, blossoms are never more ephemeral and stone never more permanent than when viewed together—the perfect harmony of opposing forces. This artful combination has captured the imagination of garden enthusiasts ever since.

Tiers of perennial colour provide a succession of blooms near this rockery wall.

SELECTING A SITE

Successful rock garden making, as with any garden design, lies in the effective use of a given site. A well-orchestrated rockery, whether a small collection of hens and chicks tucked around stones in a garden corner or a colourful tapestry of many species on a boulder-strewn slope, is one that appears unified and natural with neither plants nor stones overwhelming the effect.

The basic guidelines for creating a sturdy framework for a rock garden are the same, regardless of style and size. The first order of planning is to assess the potential of your yard to determine an appropriate site for your proposed rock garden. If your property has existing slopes and undulations, you have an ideal setting for a dramatic rockery. If your lot is completely flat, consider weaving low-growing plants and slabs of flat stone around a patio or a favourite tree. Keep in mind that rockeries are versatile design elements and are not necessarily considered separate from the rest of the yard. For example, rockeries can become an integral part of an existing water garden, bordering edges with colour while providing natural settings. They may also become an extension of a woodland wildflower planting. Rock gardens also have wonderful curb appeal, so don't overlook the potential of a front yard rockery. Above all, consider how the rock garden will be viewed from within the house or from other vantage points such as a patio or gazebo.

The orientation of the rock garden will, of course, depend on the site. Generally, it is best to choose a sunny location with some shelter from the extremes of sun and wind. An east or southeast orientation is ideal. If your rockery must face directly south, choose plants that will tolerate heat and drought conditions.

Rock gardens can take many shapes, but a curvilinear form complements most settings. Try to harmonize the rockery bed with the shape of the surrounding landscape.

Equipment and supplies may be required to build your garden, so consider access to the site—is it direct or will it damage established areas and add time and extra expense?

When selecting a site, always consider the cultural requirements of the plants. If you plan on growing specialty alpines, for example, you need to acquaint yourself with their specific cultural requirements ahead of time.

PREPARING THE SITE

For smaller rockeries, use a garden hose or rope to outline the proposed shape. Cut out the turf and remove to the recycle corner in your yard. Next, excavate the bed to a depth of about 30 cm (12"). Leave the reusable topsoil close at hand. To ensure good drainage for the plants, place about 10–20 cm (4–8") of coarse stone such as pea gravel on the base of the excavated bed. The rockery stones are placed on this firm bed and the soil is added as you progress.

SOIL

The ideal soil for your rockery depends largely on your plant selections. Soil that grows tomatoes to perfection is not, for example, the best medium for grass pinks. However, as long as the soil is well drained, many hardy plant species commonly grown in rock gardens, such as the familiar creeping phlox, are quite satisfied with a mixture of loam, sand, gravel and compost in equal parts.

The exceptions are specialty alpines. In their natural habitat, alpine plants have adapted to summer drought and extreme winter temperatures in many ways. Some formed long taproots to reach moisture hidden beneath rocky fragments. Others developed hairy leaves for protection from fluctuating temperatures or waxy leaves for maintaining a water supply. Because they evolved to suit their particular environment, alpine plants can now be difficult to grow domestically and some will not survive outside true alpine settings. But if sufficient care is given to their cultural requirements, and they do not sit in clayey soil and puddles of water, chances for survival are improved.

Specialty alpines such as mountain avens (*Dryas octopetala*) or aizoon (*Draba aizoon*) are worthy of trial and need soil full of coarse material like gravel and rock shards. This gritty mixture drains very easily. To retain at least some moisture and offer supplementary nutrients, add a bit of compost or peat moss. In addition to well-drained soil, specialty alpines require specific pH levels. The pH scale, numbered from 1 to 14, indicates the acidity or alkalinity of soil. The lower range indicates acids, 7 is neutral and the upper range indicates alkalies. Many will tolerate the midrange from 7 to 8. If you're planning an alpine rockery and you aren't certain of your soil's pH, it is a good idea to have your soil tested.

The prickly pear cactus is native to the prairies and will flourish on sandy soil in full sun.

Mountain avens bear clear white flowers in May and June. Ideal for naturalizing in sunny rockeries and well-drained soil.

SELECTING ROCKS

Choosing rocks for your garden can become a serious obsession. Whether you collect your rocks from the local quarry or from the garden site itself, you will require a strong back—remember to bend from the knees. Choose aesthetically pleasing pieces in a variety of sizes. Some weathering and a little lichen on the surface add character.

Rock gardens may be informal or natural arrangements of broken limestone or large granite boulders. They may be styled after rockslides or cliffs with flowers pouring out of cracks and seams. Whatever style you choose, the result will be most pleasing if it imitates nature as closely as possible.

When laying rock upon rock, consider using sedimentary rocks such as limestone, shale and sandstone, which have distinct parallel lines. When laying them in the garden, try to align the stratifications to simulate nature. Igneous rocks, on the other hand, make ideal accents in the rock garden. These are formed by volcanic action and often have unusual textures and colours. Lava, granite and basalt are examples. Once embedded in the rockery soil amidst attractive plants like rockcress, they mimic natural stone outcroppings.

If your tastes run to alpine gardens, model them after the accumulations of fragmented sedimentary and igneous rocks seen in screes and moraines. Scree formations are found at the bottoms of cliffs or on mountain slopes while moraines are rock deposits left by glacial action. Gathering just the right rocks for your alpine garden may be laborious work, but the effect will be worth it.

PLACING ROCKS

To calculate the amount of rock you'll need, estimate the surface area of your proposed rock garden and plan to make approximately 30–40% of it exposed rock. Working from the bottom of the rockery, place each rock on its broadest base, tilting it slightly back toward the slope so that rainwater will be shed on plant roots.

Move the rocks around until a satisfactory natural rockery design begins to appear. Then bury 1/3 to 1/2 of each rock. Crevices between closely grouped rocks are ideal locations for some tiny alpine plants. To add variety and interest, a rock here and there can be split with a hammer. Exercise caution and always use protective eyewear.

As you fill in the spaces around the rocks with soil, leave no air pockets for unsuspecting roots to find later on. Try to allow for a soil depth of at least 30 cm (12").

SELECTING ROCKERY PLANTS

The most attractive rock gardens have something colourful and interesting flowering from early spring until late autumn. Choose from a variety of perennials, dwarf flowering bulbs, dwarf shrubs and vines, and even ornamental grasses. The many colours and textures of rockery plant foliage can also add interest.

Perennials give rock gardens their essential character. At the

Magenta maiden pinks tumble over rocks beside sedums, grass pinks, thyme and misty mounds of snow-in-summer. These rockery plants thrive in full sun and well-drained soil.

For spring colour in the rock garden, plant grape hyacinths. They are particularly attractive beside yellow early flowering tulips.

back of a sloping rock garden in spring, the blue spurred flowers and graceful foliage of alpine columbine (*Aquilegia alpina*) beside pink flowering geum (*Geum triflorum*) will occasion a soft casual mood. In the front, drifts of magenta and white flowering creeping phlox (*Phlox subulata*) will spill cheerful colour over a rockery path. As spring blossoms fade, the colours of the rock garden can change from subtle pastels to calypso shades of summer. The silken orange petals of Iceland poppies (*Papaver nudicaule*) look stunning next to Purple Haze bearded tongue (*Penstemon fruticosus* 'Purple Haze'). At their feet, bellflowers (*Campanula* spp.), thyme (*Thymus* spp.) and stonecrop (*Sedum* spp.) can compete for empty space between rocks. Enjoying full sun and well-drained soil in many rock gardens is creeping baby's breath (*Gypsophila repens*). With small leaves and tiny white flowers, it is a perfect low companion to the rosy magenta flowers of clammy campion (*Lychnis viscaria* 'Splendens Flore-pleno').

From early spring irises (*Iris reticulata*) and miniature tulips (*Tulipa* spp.) to anemones (*Anemone* spp.) and cheerful squills (*Scilla* spp.), many bulbs are suitable for pocket plantings in the rock garden. Be sure to plant these treasures where their delicate beauty can easily be seen. In my rock garden, the showy parade of colour begins with the tiny violet-blue blos-

Maiden pinks seed with weedlike abandon. After flowering, shear their flower stems to make the foliage more attractive.

soms of early spring iris (*Iris reticulata*) and mauve-blue grape hyacinths (*Muscari botryoides*). Soon the rosy pink of the 'Peach Blossom' tulip emerges from behind grey slabs of limestone. The scented white flowers of perennial candytuft (*Iberis sempervirens*) complement this spring picture. When planning your rock garden, remember that shorter flowering bulbs are more suited to rockeries than taller varieties. You can choose from an extensive list of hybridized bulbs that produce a variety of single and double forms, but the *Tulipa tarda,* a native of Turkestan, is considered an exceptional species choice. It bears bright yellow and white star-shaped blossoms.

Sedums are low-growing succulent plants with attractive foliage and colourful flowers. Well suited for rockeries in hot dry locations.

Alberta gardeners can also choose from a wide variety of deciduous shrubs and vines ideally suited to rockery conditions. Consider the hardy spirea (*Spiraea* spp.), the prolific flowering broom (*Genista* spp.), the scented ground clematis (*Clematis recta*) and the weeping form of Walker caragana (*Caragana arborescens* 'Walker'). With its unusual brightly coloured seed capsule, the dwarf narrow leaved burning bush (*Euonymus nana* 'Turkestanica') is also an impressive addition.

Perhaps your rockery has room for some attractive horizontal junipers (*Juniperus horizontalis*) or dwarf mugo pines (*Pinus mugo* 'Teeny' or 'Compacta'). You might also try the dwarf cultivar of Colorado blue spruce (*Picea pungens* 'Glauca'), which offers bright blue colour and a creeping growth habit, or the low-growing nest spruce (*Picea abies*

This canvas of rock garden colour incorporates a variety of textures, forms and heights to create a beautiful scene. Vibrant-coloured grass pinks complement moss phlox, snow-in-summer, maiden pinks and other sun-loving perennials.

Many gardeners, while waiting for young rock garden perennials to become established, fill in empty spaces with low-growing annuals. With the assistance of cascading petunias, alyssum, lobelia and portulaca, colourful rock gardens can be enjoyed quickly.

'Nidiformis'), which has an unusual bowl-shaped form.

While most gardens can support a wide selection of ornamental grasses, a few of the hardier varieties—with their unique forms and textures—are more appropriate for Alberta rock gardens. Sheep's fescue (*Festuca ovina* var. *glauca*), for example, is one of the most popular and attractive accent grasses. It enjoys full sun and is particularly stunning when planted en masse.

CREATING AN ALPINE TROUGH GARDEN

For something out of the ordinary, consider a miniature alpine rockery in a stone trough of the sort once used on farms. When transforming a stone trough, you'll need to drill drainage holes with a masonry drill. Fill the trough to a few inches below the rim with a prepared soil mix containing equal parts of pasteurized soil, peat moss and coarse sand and rock particles. For some specialty alpine species, you will need a mix containing a higher ratio of sand and rock particles.

Depending on plant and trough size, you will need in the region of 10–20 plants. Many miniature rock garden species are suitable for trough plantings in both sun and partial shade. If you prefer, the entire trough garden can consist of one species. For example, sun-loving hens and chicks (*Sempervivum* spp.) or stonecrops (*Sedum* spp.) come in a variety of shapes and colours. The soft pink

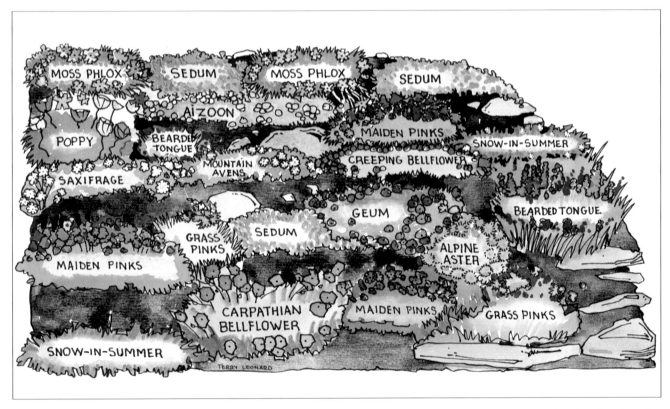

The key to designing beguiling rock gardens is the harmonious integration of design elements. As this design illustrates, the delicate plant forms in rock gardens offer gentle rhythms of colour and texture spilling over stone.

flowers of pussytoes (*Antennaria rosea*), which stand above a mat of grey-green leaves, make an interesting display either planted alone or with the bright pink flowers of Arctic phlox (*Phlox borealis*) as a sun-loving companion.

If your trough is located in shade, the perennial creeping jenny (*Lysimachia nummularia*) will form a cascading carpet of round leaves and bright golden flowers in late spring. Primroses (*Primula* spp.) when planted e*n masse* are also well suited for shaded trough gardens.

Once planting is completed, cover the soil with rock shards to conserve moisture and discourage weeds. Ensure adequate water is provided for the choices you have selected. Regular maintenance is required during the growing season.

THE ROCK GARDEN

COMMON NAME	BOTANICAL NAME	HEIGHT	SPREAD
Sunny Rock Garden Perennials			
Stonecress	Aethionema spp.	10–30 cm (4–12")	30 cm (12")
Anenome	Anemone spp.	20–40 cm (8–16")	varies
European Pasque Flower	Anemone pulsatilla	20–40 cm (8–16")	20 cm (8")
Pussytoes	Antennaria rosea	5–20 cm (2–8")	5–20 cm (2–8")
Alpine Columbine	Aquilegia alpina	20–30 cm (8–12")	30 cm (12")
Wild Red Columbine	Aquilegia canadensis	60 cm (24")	35–45 cm (14–18")
Japanese Columbine	Aquilegia flabellata 'Alba'	20–30 cm (8–12")	varies
Rockcress	Arabis alpina	15–20 cm (6–8")	30–40 cm (12–16")
Sea Pinks	Armeria maritima	10–30 cm (4–12")	10–30 cm (4–12")
Silver Mound Artemisia	Artemisia schmidtiana 'Silver Mound'	30 cm (12")	30–45 cm (12–18")
Alpine Aster	Aster alpinus	20–25 cm (8–10")	20–30 cm (8–12")
Basket-of-Gold	Aurinia saxatilis	25–30 cm (10–12")	25–30 cm (10–12")
Snow-in-Summer	Cerastium tomentosum	15 cm (6")	varies
Maiden Pinks	Dianthus deltoides	15–20 cm (6–8")	30–45 cm (12–18")
Grass Pinks	Dianthus plumarius	40 cm (16")	30 cm (12")
Shooting Star	Dodecatheon meadia	30 cm (12")	15 cm (6")
Aizoon	Draba aizoon	10 cm (4")	varies
Mountain Avens	Dryas octopetala	5–20 cm (2–8")	varies
Cushion Spurge	Euphorbia 'Polychroma'	30–45 cm (12–18")	45–55 cm (18–22")
Sheep's Fescue	Festuca ovina var. glauca	20–30 cm (8–12")	30–45 cm (12–18")
Cranesbill Geranium	Geranium sanguineum	30 cm (12")	30 cm (12")
Geum	Geum triflorum	30 cm (12")	30 cm (12")
Creeping Baby's Breath	Gypsophila repens	10–15 cm (4–6")	45–60 cm (18–24")
Stella d'Oro Daylily	Hemerocallis 'Stella d'Oro'	30 cm (12")	varies
Coralbells	Heuchera spp.	30–75 cm (12–30")	30 cm (12")
Perennial Candytuft	Iberis sempervirens	30 cm (12")	30–50 cm (12–20")
Arctic Iris	Iris setosa	15–20 cm (6–8")	30 cm (12")
Alpine Edelweiss	Leontopodium alpinum	15 cm (6")	25 cm (10")
Perennial Flax	Linum perenne	25–30 cm (10–12")	30–45 cm (12–18")
Arctic Campion	Lychnis alpina	10–15 cm (4–6")	15 cm (6")
Clammy Campion	Lychnis viscaria 'Splendens Flore-pleno'	30–45 cm (12–18")	30 cm (12")
Iceland Poppy	Papaver nudicaule	30–40 cm (12–16")	30–40 cm (12–16")
Purple Haze Bearded Tongue	Penstemon fruticosus 'Purple Haze'	20 cm (8")	60 cm (24")
Arctic Phlox	Phlox borealis	5–10 cm (2–4")	30 cm (12")
Creeping Phlox	Phlox subulata	10–15 cm (4–6")	30–45 cm (12–18")
Saxifrage	Saxifraga spp.	8–15 cm (3–6")	varies
Stonecrop	Sedum spp.	10–60 cm (4–24")	30–60 cm (12–24")
Hens and Chicks	Sempervivum spp.	2.5–10 cm (1–4")	15–30 cm (6–12")
Moss Campion	Silene acaulis	2.5 cm (1")	15–30 cm (6–12")
Thyme	Thymus spp.	varies	varies
Veronica	Veronica spp.	2.5–45 cm (1–18")	varies

FOLIAGE COLOUR	FLOWER COLOUR	COMMENTS
green	pink, purple, white	masses of tiny blooms
grey, green	white, mauve	early spring blooms
grey green	mauve	early spring blooms
grey	rose	mat forming
green	bright blue	prolific display of delicate blooms
green	red	best in woodland rockeries
green	white	delicate spurred blooms
grey green	pink, white	creeping, fragrant
green	carmine, pink, white	grassy foliage, pom-pomlike blooms
silver grey	yellow	accent plant
green	pink, blue, white	good display of daisylike blooms
green	yellow	bright, cheerful mass of blooms
grey	white	mat forming, contrast plant
blue green to bronze	carmine, pink, white	mat forming, masses of blooms
green	rose, pink, salmon, white	scented blooms, grassy foliage
green	rose, pink	best as border plant
green	yellow	early flowering
green	white	creeping evergreen
green	yellow	unusual blooms
blue green	inconspicuous	accent plant
green	magenta	ground cover
green	pink	interesting seed pods
green	pink, white	masses of tiny blooms
green	yellow	dwarf, repeat bloomer
varies	red, pink, white	sprays of delicate blooms
green	white	mat forming
green	lavender	mass of colour
silver grey	white	starlike blooms
green	blue, white	delicate blooms
green	pink	clusters of bright pink blooms
green	magenta	sticky stems, delicate sprays of blooms
green	wide variety	self-seeds readily
green	lilac purple	cascading colour
green	pink	mat forming
green	red, pink, blue, white	mat forming
green	pink, white	tuftlike form, dainty blooms
varies	varies	extensive flower and foliage types
varies	varies	succulents, starlike flowers
green	pink	cushions of greenery
varies	varies	aromatic, mat forming
green, grey	pink, blue, white	extensive variety of flower and foliage

COMMON NAME	BOTANICAL NAME	HEIGHT	SPREAD
Shady Rock Garden Perennials			
Carpet Bugleweed	*Ajuga reptans*	10 cm (4")	30–45 cm (12–18")
Golden Columbine	*Aquilegia chyrsantha*	45–75 cm (18–30")	30–45 cm (12–18")
Bergenia	*Bergenia cordifolia*	30–45 cm (12–18")	varies
Bellflower	*Campanula* spp.	varies	varies
Lily-of-the-Valley	*Convallaria majalis*	10–20 cm (4–8")	varies
Mountain Gentian	*Gentiana acaulis*	10 cm (4")	30 cm (12")
Hosta	*Hosta* spp.	30–90 cm (12–36")	varies
Creeping Jenny	*Lysimachia nummularia*	10 cm (4")	45 cm (18")
Primrose	*Primula* spp.	varies	varies
Periwinkle	*Vinca minor*	10–15 cm (4–6")	30–45 cm (12–18")
Dwarf Shrubs and Vines			
Walker Caragana	*Caragana arborescens* 'Walker'	varies	varies
Ground Clematis	*Clematis recta*	1–1.5 M (3–5')	1–1.5 M (3–5')
Rock Garden Broom	*Cytisus decumbens* 'Vancouver Gold'	50 cm (20")	1 M (3')
Dwarf Narrow Leaved Burning Bush	*Euonymus nana* 'Turkestanica'	60 cm (24")	1 M (3')
Woadwaxen	*Genista* spp.	60 cm (24")	varies
Lydia Woadwaxen	*Genista lydia*	60 cm (24")	1M (3')
Engelman's Virginia Creeper	*Parthenocissus quinquefolia* 'Engelmannii'	15–20 M (49–66')	5 M (16')
Spirea	*Spiraea* spp.	50 cm–2 M (1.5–7')	varies
Crispa Spirea	*Spiraea* x *bumalda* 'Crispa'	50 cm (20")	50 cm (20")
Gold Flame Spirea	*Spiraea* x *bumalda* 'Gold Flame'	1 M (3')	1 M (3')
Dwarf Evergreens			
Horizontal Juniper	*Juniperus horizontalis*	60 cm–1 M (2–3')	varies
Blue Chip Juniper	*Juniperus horizontalis* 'Blue Chip'	15–25 cm (6–10")	1 M (3')
Prince of Wales Juniper	*Juniperus horizontalis* 'Prince of Wales'	15–25 cm (6–10")	2–3 M (7–10')
Calgary Carpet Juniper	*Juniperus sabina* 'Calgary Carpet'	1 M (3')	2 M (7')
Nest Spruce	*Picea abies* 'Nidiformis'	1 M (3')	1.5 M (5')
Dwarf Mugo Pine	*Pinus mugo* 'Compacta'	1 M (3')	1 M (3')
Dwarf Mugo Pine	*Pinus mugo* 'Teeny'	30–60 cm (12–24")	30–60 cm (12–24")
Colorado Blue Spruce	*Picea pungens* 'Glauca'	50 cm (20")	varies
Bulbs and Others			
Blue Globe Onion	*Allium caeruleum*	60 cm (24")	varies
Ostrowsky Onion	*Allium ostrowskianum*	15 cm (6")	varies
Glory-of-the-Snow	*Chionodoxa* spp.	15–25 cm (6–10")	varies
Autumn Crocus	*Colchicum* spp.	20–30 cm (8–12")	varies
Crocus	*Crocus* spp.	10–15 cm (4–6")	varies
Fritillaria	*Fritillaria pallidiflora*	30–45 cm (12–18")	varies
Danfordiae Iris	*Iris danfordiae*	10–15 cm (4–6")	varies
Early Spring Iris	*Iris reticulata*	10–15 cm (4–6")	varies
Bearded Iris	*Iris* x *germanica*	varies	varies
Asiatic Lily	*Lilium* spp.	30–90 cm (12–36")	varies
Grape Hyacinth	*Muscari* spp.	10–20 cm (4–8")	varies
Daffodil	*Narcissus* spp.	15–45 cm (6–18")	varies
Squill	*Scilla* spp.	10–15 cm (4–6")	varies
Tulip	*Tulipa* spp.	5–60 cm (2–24")	varies
Tulip	*Tulipa* 'Peach Blossom'	30 cm (12")	varies
Tulip	*Tulipa tarda*	5–10 cm (2–4")	varies

FOLIAGE COLOUR	FLOWER COLOUR	COMMENTS
varies	blue	mat forming
green	yellow	large spurred blooms
green	red, pink, white	large glossy leaves, winter colour
green	blue, purple, white	many shapes and sizes
green	white	scented bell-shaped blooms
green	blue	trumpet-shaped flowers
varies	lavender, white	exotic foliage
green	yellow	invasive, mat forming
green	wide variety	delicate blooms, some species and cultivars scented
green, variegated	blue, purple, white	ground cover
green	yellow	weeping form, good accent
green	white	scented vine
green	yellow	bright profuse blooms
green	yellow	unusual capsule, good autumn colour
green	yellow	colourful pealike flowers
green	yellow	outstanding dwarf flowering shrub
green	inconspicuous	spectacular autumn colour, good for reclamation
green	white, pink	some cultivars suitable in rockeries
reddish green	rosy pink	interesting foliage
reddish gold	dull pink	showy en masse, good accent
varies	inconspicuous	wide variety of form and foliage colour
blue	inconspicuous	one of the best blue junipers
blue green	inconspicuous	good ground cover, winter interest
green	inconspicuous	excellent form
green	not applicable	unique bowl shape
green	not applicable	dense globular shape
dark green	inconspicuous	nice form, good contrast
blue green	inconspicuous	interesting growth habit
green	blue	attractive globe bloom
green	pink	attractive pink blooms
green	pink, blue, white	early delicate spring blooms
green	pink, purple, mauve, white	late season colour
green	wide variety	good for naturalizing, delightful spring colour
blue green	mint green	striking blooms, good accent,
green	yellow	perfect in rockeries
green	wide variety	scented blooms
green	wide variety	rainbow of colours
green	wide variety	stunning late season colour, good accent
green	blue, purple, white	thick carpet of colour
green	pink, orange, yellow, cream, white	brilliant colours
green	blue, white	good for naturalizing
green	wide variety	showy blooms
green	pink	large double blooms
green	yellow and white	star-shaped spring blooms

THE SHADE GARDEN

*"The first purpose of a garden is to give
happiness and repose of mind"*

–Gertrude Jekyll

Beneath the branches of mature trees or in the shadowy nooks of buildings or fences are the true hidden treasures of the garden. These gloomy pockets are frequently neglected because many gardeners assume that plants can't thrive there. But don't be afraid of the dark. With a bit of imagination shady areas can become festivals of colour or tranquil retreats. Pink and white bleeding hearts, mauve-blue Siberian irises, curiously spurred columbines, sea-green hostas, woodland wildflowers, colourful clematis and winged burning bush are only a few of the many jewels at their best in Alberta shade.

Lush green ostrich ferns offer an enticing background for a carpet of goutweed while mature spruces extend an invitation to explore this dense-shade garden further.

Besides bringing colour and form to frequently neglected parts of the yard, shade gardens offer several other distinct advantages. Shade-loving plants have a lower metabolic rate and thus need less water that their sun-worshipping cousins. Their flowers emerge at a more leisurely pace and provide vibrant colour for longer periods. Better still, most weeds and heat-loving insects, such as spider mites, avoid the shade. And for their efforts, gardeners are rewarded with a refreshingly cool bower to enjoy in the heat of midsummer.

CLASSIFYING SHADE

Successful shade gardening depends on selecting plants suitable for the conditions present. In any given garden, the amount of available light will vary from morning to dusk, from day to day and from week to week throughout the growing season. To identify the type of shade in your garden, tour the site at about two-hour intervals on a sunny day early in the summer and note the pattern of available light. Remember that even without a single tree, parts of your garden will probably still be shaded by neighbouring trees and structures for at least a portion of the day.

Shade is a relative term. To help distinguish one shade pattern from another, several adjectives are used. *Dappled* or *partial shade* best describes the drifting pattern of light and shadow under trees, such as birch, which have open or airy canopies. This type of shade offers the brightest spectrum of light and supports the broadest range of plants.

Alternate shade shifts from sun to shade or vice versa according to the time of day. The critical factor is when each dominates the garden. Some plants, for example, tolerate morning sun but need cool shade in the afternoon.

Dense shade, on the other hand, consists of an almost complete lack of available light. This typically occurs when buildings and mature trees stand shoulder to shoulder and block the light for all but a few hours before sunset. Here, the plant selection is somewhat limited, but with careful planning, a shady paradise is still possible.

SELECTING AND PREPARING A SITE

Light—or lack of it—is only one criterion that determines how plants will flourish. Before you buy a single columbine or ostrich fern for your shady garden, check the condition of your soil. A soil that drains quickly is ideal because it prevents overwatering, which can lead to mildew or other annoying fungi. Fortunately, soil is the one element most amenable to change. Simply spread 5–10 cm (2–4") of damp peat moss and about 5 cm (2") of compost, and dig the mixture in deeply; then rake to a fine surface.

If you are developing a shade garden beneath a stand of trees, you may need to raise the soil level by about 5–10 cm (2–4"). This will give the plants room to grow and will reduce competition from tree root systems. Soil containing a high content of decayed or organic matter is ideal for shade-loving plants.

Beneath the canopy of a mature mountain ash and weeping birch is a shady woodland paradise, inviting respite from a hot sunny day.

SHADY WOODLAND GARDENS

The growing appeal of designing gardens with wildflowers is easy to understand. Wildflowers offer understatement rather than bold drama. Shady nooks and crannies are ideal places to feature some of the our most unusual and beautiful wild species. Although we cannot perfectly recreate the complex natural shady woodland habitat, we nevertheless can draw inspiration from it and design gardens that evoke the same casual natural grace. But purchase nursery-grown plants and leave nature's wildflowers for the enjoyment of all. Fortunately, Alberta has many nurserymen and plantsmen dedicated to making Alberta's finest wildflowers widely available.

The dappled shade of a stand of birches or trembling aspens, both native species in themselves, is an ideal location for creating a miniature woodland area overflowing with wildflowers. But whether your trees are native species or not, you can still plant a variety of woodland flowers beneath them, right up to their trunks, provided enough shade is cast.

Among the best choices for this partial shade woodland garden are the Canada anemone (*Anemone canadensis*), with its showy, white cup-shaped flowers, and the wild columbine (*Aquilegia brevistyla*), an attractive companion with blue and cream nodding blooms. Another attractive Alberta wildflower suitable for shady woodland gardens is the low-growing bunchberry (*Cornus canadensis*). This charming little plant has a whorl of four white petal-like bracts surrounding a tiny cluster of true flowers. A white flowering perennial at home in the shade garden is trillium (*Trillium ovatum*), a rare but attractive Alberta wildflower that produces single white flowers bearing three petals and three green sepals above three leaves in early spring. Consider bordering your wildflower garden with the western wood lily (*Lilium philadelphicum* var. *andinum*). This much-loved species grows throughout our province in a variety of places from moist meadows to shady woodlands. The orange-red flowers are borne on erect stems reaching 30–60 cm (1–2') in height. For moist locations consider a dense planting of spring-blooming primroses (*Primula* spp.).

Ferns, with their fancy fronds and delicate airy tassels, add an ethereal quality to dense shade conditions. According to one garden writer, ferns "put wings on the garden." Try ostrich ferns (*Matteuccia struthiopteris*) *en masse* in a deep shade corner or as a companion to trillium (*Trillium ovatum*) or lily-of-the-valley (*Convallaria majalis*), which produces tiny bell-shaped blooms in spring.

SHADY ANNUAL GARDENS

By definition, *annuals* are plants that grow from seed through flowering to seed production in a single growing season. A short life indeed. Yet, despite their lifespan, they offer the creative gardener a generous portfolio, especially for those shady nooks and crannies where containers represent the best option.

In dappled shade locations, tuberous begonias (*Begonia* x *tuberhybrida*) radiate show-stopping colours from the shadows. They are especially attractive when paired with cascading Kennelworth ivy (*Cymbalaria* spp.). For a subtler statement, choose Martha Washington geraniums (*Pelargonium* x *domesticum*), available in a variety of soft pastels, and fuchsias (*Fuchsia* spp.), with their crowds of arabesque blooms.

Most gardens have at least one pocket of dense shade. To fill it with colour, add cheerful blue pansies (*Viola* spp.) grouped near magenta pink impatiens (*Impatiens wallerana*) planted *en masse*. Crowded

Ostrich ferns, with their gracefully arching fronds, make an attractive green companion for this horizontal juniper.

earthen pots of these showy annuals are perfect for summer colour in shady corners of decks or patios.

SHADY PERENNIAL GARDENS

Unlike annuals, perennials can live several years and, in many cases, a lifetime. Technically, *herbaceous perennials* are nonwoody ornamental plants that die back to ground level each winter and produce new top growth each spring. A vast assortment of hardy perennials are suitable for Alberta shade gardens.

Without doubt, one of the most valuable perennials for partial shade gardens is the bleeding heart (*Dicentra spectablis*). Its only shortcoming is that its foliage dies back after its profuse spring blooming. Wise gardeners camouflage the unsightly foliage with shorter companion plants in front. Both daylily (*Hemerocallis* spp.) and bellflower (*Campanula* spp.) are excellent choices.

For dense shade locations try the hardy and dependable bergenia (*Bergenia cordifolia*). Easily recognized by its spikes of rosy purple flowers and large cabbagelike leaves, it adds dramatic textural interest, especially when planted in masses beneath a dense tree canopy. A more delicate effect is achieved with a carpet of lily-of-the-valley (*Convallaria majalis*), which has the added virtue of providing perfumed blooms in spring.

SHADY VERTICAL GARDENS

Even the smallest of shade gardens has room to expand vertically. In these environments, explore the potential of shade-tolerant climbing plants, which will soften the hard lines of fences and walls.

One of the most reliable of Alberta climbers is the

Tuberous begonias will brighten virtually any shady corner. Available in colours and forms to suit every garden palette.

Virginia creeper (*Parthenocissus quinquefolia*). It is a master climber, creeping up walls and fences with tendrils that wrap themselves around anything near. The cultivar 'Englemannii' has adhesive pads that fasten themselves to vertical surfaces. Although its stunning autumn colour isn't quite as spectacular in shady places, the Virginia creeper is still an attractive adornment for fences, walls and arbors in dappled shade where it will reach heights of 15–20 M (50–65'). The decision to plant the Virginia creeper should not be taken lightly—once established, this climber tends to be aggressive. And its tolerance to wind and drought—and even a busy gardener's benign neglect—make it difficult to get rid of once established.

Another ideal hardy climbing vine is the dropmore scarlet trumpet honeysuckle (*Lonicera* x *brownii* 'Dropmore Scarlet Trumpet'). Developed in Manitoba, this flowering vine is perfect for east-facing arbors and fences. It produces pairs of bright orange trumpet-shaped flowers in the axils (the upper angle formed by the leaf and stem) of the leaves. Trumpet honeysuckle vines reach a mature height of approximately 3 M (10'). Gardens sporting trumpet honeysuckle are also an invitation for hummingbirds.

Clematis (*Clematis* spp.), the queen of climbers, is excellent for locations where the roots can stay cool and shaded. With this cultural requirement met, clematis will bloom prolifically when draped over a hedge or in its more traditional location—adorning an arbor. The golden rule for success with clematis is cool roots and warm tops. Even on an east-facing wall, clematis provides brilliant summer colour. Among the several species of clematis, Jackmann's is a popular, deep purple flowering hybrid. This colourful climber blooms on new wood from the bottom to the top of the vine. The hardy 'Ville de Lyon' also blooms on new wood bearing large rosy red flowers. Both of these need to be cut back to 15 cm (6") from the base in the autumn and watered heavily once the ground starts to freeze.

Other species of clematis include the golden virgin's bower (*Clematis tangutica*) and the big petal clematis (*Clematis macropetala*). The golden virgin's bower, with its bright yellow flowers, is especially appealing draped over an old fence bordering a woodland garden or training up a tree. Both are vigorous growers and can reach heights of 2 M (6') in a single year. Both bloom on old and new wood in May and June, and occasionally again in late August. For more prolific blooms next season, prune them when flowering is finished for the season.

SHADY SHRUB GARDENS

At one time in the evolution of gardens, shrubs were not considered an integral part of design. Today, wise gardeners have come to depend on them to perform a variety of important roles. Shrubbery softens the transition between tall garden elements like buildings and trees. In small urban gardens, shrubs provide gradations of height, effectively framing pleasant views and hiding unsightly ones. Shrubs with vigorous root systems may also inhibit erosion. Besides their practical function, they produce many aesthetic effects including seasonal bloom, richly coloured foliage and attractive fruit and berries.

Because shrubs perform transitional roles, they often find themselves on the shady sides of buildings and taller trees. One of the most popular shrub species for the shady garden is the dogwood (*Cornus* spp.).

With arabesque blooms dancing from their stems, fuchsias are ideal in dappled shade.

A particularly striking form is the tartarian silver-leaved dogwood (*Cornus alba* 'Argenteo-marginata'), which brightens up shady corners with its variegated white and green leaves. It is particularly showy beside a dense planting of clustered bellflower (*Campanula glomerata*) or Siberian iris (*Iris sibirica*). The silver-leaved dogwood reaches a mature height of 1–1.5 M (3–4.5') and is globular in form. Another dogwood cultivar is 'Aurea' (*Cornus alba* 'Aurea'). Its yellow-green leaves provide lovely contrast against brown or natural wood fences. For a shrub that does double duty, consider the Siberian coral dogwood (*Cornus alba* 'Sibirica'). Its bright coral-red stems are attractive near evergreens and provide dramatic winter interest.

A small shrub to consider for a splash of autumn colour in partial shade is the winged burning bush (*Euonymus alatus*). With a mature height of approximately 1 M (3') and an upright spreading form, this hardy shrub turns deep pink in autumn and offers small unusual fruit. The cultivar 'Compactus' is also attractive but smaller and neater in appearance. In front of larger shrubs or as dwarf hedges, both are ideal for partial shade.

Without a doubt, the hardy saskatoon (*Amelanchier alnifolia*) is also suitable for partial shade. While it is grown chiefly for its fruit, it is well worth considering as an ornamental shrub. The 'Pembina' and 'Smoky' cultivars, developed here in Alberta, are popular choices. These large flowering shrubs reach heights of approximately 3 M (10') and look attractive against garage walls or near fences or arbors. They are especially attractive in spring when they are smothered in blooms.

Create a hidden paradise brimming with lush ferns, scented daylilies and charming columbine. Alberta gardeners can choose from a wide variety of shade-tolerant plants to nurture their own shady retreat.

The next time you wander your garden in search of inspiration for new developments, look into the nooks and crannies you've passed by before. They are your garden's hidden potential. Imagine a shady bower of shrubs, vines and flowers with a small stone, wood or wrought iron bench, and then start to work. When the heat of the summer drives you out of the sun, you'll be glad you did.

THE SHADE GARDEN

COMMON NAME	BOTANICAL NAME	HEIGHT	SPREAD
Shade Tolerant Shrubs and Vines			
Saskatoon	*Amelanchier alnifolia*	3 M (10')	2 M (7')
Pembina Saskatoon	*Amelanchier alnifolia* 'Pembina'	3 M (10')	2 M (7')
Smoky Saskatoon	*Amelanchier alnifolia* 'Smoky'	3 M (10')	2 M (7')
Clematis	*Clematis* spp.	1–4 M (3–13')	varies
Big Petal Clematis	*Clematis macropetala*	2 M (7')	2 M (7')
Golden Virgin's Bower	*Clematis tangutica*	3 M (10')	2 M (7')
Ville de Lyon Clematis	*Clematis* 'Ville de Lyon'	4 M (13')	2 M (7')
Jackmann's Clematis	*Clematis x jackmannii*	4 M (13')	2 M (7')
Dogwood	*Cornus* spp.	1–2 M (3–7')	1–2 M (3–7')
Tartarian Silver-Leaved Dogwood	*Cornus alba* 'Argenteo-marginata'	1 M (3')	1 M (3')
Aurea Dogwood	*Cornus alba* 'Aurea'	1 M (3')	1 M (3')
Siberian Coral Dogwood	*Cornus alba* 'Sibirica'	1 M (3')	1 M (3')
Beaked Hazelnut	*Corylus cornuta*	2 M (7')	1 M (3')
Winged Burning Bush	*Euonymus alata*	1 M (3')	1 M (3')
Dwarf Winged Burning Bush	*Euonymus alata* 'Compactus'	75 cm (30")	75 cm (30")
Pee Gee Hydrangea	*Hydrangea paniculata* 'Grandiflora'	1 M (3')	1 M (3')
Dropmore Scarlet Trumpet Honeysuckle	*Lonicera x brownii* 'Dropmore Scarlet Trumpet'	2–3 M (7–10')	1M (3')
Engelman's Virginia Creeper	*Parthenocissus quinquefolia* 'Englemannii'	15–20 M (49–66')	varies
Nanking Cherry	*Prunus tomentosa*	2 M (7')	2 M (7')
Red Elder	*Sambucus racemosa*	3 M (10')	3 M (10')
Russet Buffaloberry	*Shepherdia canadensis*	3 M (10')	2 M (7')
Meyer Lilac	*Syringa meyeri*	2 M (7')	2 M (7')
Manchurian Lilac	*Syringa velutina*	3 M (10')	3 M (10')
American Highbush Cranberry	*Viburnum trilobum*	3 M (10')	1.5 M (5')
Shade Tolerant Annuals			
Fibrous Begonia	*Begonia x semerflorens cultorum*	10–15 cm (4–6")	5 cm (2")
Tuberous Begonia	*Begonia x tuberhybrida*	20–45 cm (8–18")	20–25 cm (8–10")
Ornamental Kale	*Brassica oleracea*	30–50 cm (12–20")	30 cm (12")
Browallia	*Browallia speciosa*	30 cm (12")	15 cm (6")
Dracena	*Cordyline indivisa*	50–90 cm (20–36")	30–60 cm (12–24")
Kennelworth Ivy	*Cymbalaria* spp.	5 cm (2")	varies
Sweet William	*Dianthus barbatus*	15–30 cm (6–12")	15–30 cm (6–12")
Fuchsia	*Fuchsia* spp.	varies	varies
Impatiens	*Impatiens wallerana*	10–30 cm (4–12")	10–30 cm (4–12")
Lobelia	*Lobelia erinus*	10–15 cm (4–6")	10–20 cm (4–8")
Nicotiana	*Nicotiana alata*	25–40 cm (10–16")	15 cm (6")
Ivy Geranium	*Pelargonium peltatum*	varies	varies
Martha Washington Geranium	*Pelargonium x domesticum*	30–45 cm (12–18")	varies
Butterfly Flower	*Schizanthus x wisetonensis*	30–60 cm (12–24")	20 cm (8")
Pansy	*Viola* spp.	10–15 cm (4–6")	10–20 cm (4–8")

FOLIAGE COLOUR	FLOWER COLOUR	COMMENTS
green	white	partial shade
green	white	partial shade
green	white	partial shade
green	wide variety	partial shade
green	violet	partial shade
green	yellow	partial shade
green	red	partial shade
green	wide variety	partial shade
varies	white	partial to dense shade
variegated green and white	white	partial shade
variegated green and yellow	white	partial shade
green	white	partial shade
green	inconspicuous	partial shade
green	yellow	partial shade
green	yellow	partial shade
green	pink	partial to dense shade
green	orange	partial shade
green	inconspicuous	partial shade, excellent climber
green	pink	partial shade
green	white	interesting texture
dull green	yellow	partial shade
green	pink	partial shade, fragrant
green	blue	partial shade, fragrant
green	white	partial shade, good autumn colour
green to bronze	red, pink, white	partial to dense shade
green	wide variety	partial shade, morning sun only
varies	yellow	partial shade
dark green	blue	partial shade
green	white	partial shade
green	mauve	partial to dense shade
green	red, pink, white, bicolour	partial shade
green, bronze	wide variety	partial shade, morning sun only
green, bronze	wide variety	partial to dense shade
green, bronze	carmine, blue, white	partial shade
green	varies	partial shade
green	wide variety	partial shade
green	wide variety	partial shade
green	wide variety	partial shade
green	wide variety	partial to dense shade

COMMON NAME	BOTANICAL NAME	HEIGHT	SPREAD
Shade Tolerant Perennials			
Carpet Bugleweed	*Ajuga reptans*	15 cm (6")	30–45 cm (12–18")
Canada Anemone	*Anemone canadensis*	20 cm (8")	varies
Snowdrop Anemone	*Anemone sylvestris*	30–45 cm (12–18")	30–45 cm (12–18")
Columbine	*Aquilegia* spp.	30–60 cm (12–24")	30–60 cm (12–24")
Wild Columbine	*Aquilegia brevistyla*	30–60 cm (12–24")	varies
Dwarf Chinese Astilbe	*Astilbe chinensis* 'Pumila'	30 cm (12")	30 cm (12")
Bergenia	*Bergenia cordifolia*	30–45 cm (12–18")	varies
Bellflower	*Campanula* spp.	varies	varies
Clustered Bellflower	*Campanula glomerata*	60 cm (24")	varies
Lily-of-the-Valley	*Convallaria majalis*	10–20 cm (4–8")	varies
Bunchberry	*Cornus canadensis*	10 cm (4")	varies
Sweet William	*Dianthus barbatus*	30–60 cm (12–24")	varies
Bleeding Heart	*Dicentra spectablis*	90 cm (36")	30–60 cm (12–24")
Sheep's Fescue	*Festuca ovina* var. *glauca*	20–30 cm (8–12")	30–45 cm (12–18")
Mountain Gentian	*Gentiana acaulis*	10 cm (4")	30 cm (12")
Daylily	*Hemerocallis* spp.	varies	varies
Hosta	*Hosta* spp.	30–90 cm (12–36")	varies
Siberian Iris	*Iris sibirica*	60 cm–1.2 M (2–4')	varies
Spotted Deadnettle	*Lamium maculatum*	5–10 cm (2–4")	varies
Elephant Ears	*Ligularia* spp.	1–1.2 M (3–4')	varies
Western Wood Lily	*Lilium philadelphicum* var. *andinum*	30–60 cm (12–24")	varies
Creeping Jenny	*Lysimachia nummularia*	10 cm (4")	45 cm (18")
Ostrich Fern	*Matteuccia struthiopteris*	1–1.5 M (3–5')	varies
Virginia Bluebells	*Mertensia virginica*	60 cm (24")	30 cm (12")
Forget-Me-Not	*Myosotis sylvatica*	30 cm (12")	30 cm (12")
Bearded Tongue	*Penstemon* spp.	30–90 cm (12–36")	varies
Balloonflower	*Platycodon grandiflorum*	45–60 cm (18–24")	30 cm (12")
Solomon's Seal	*Polygonatum multiflorum*	75 cm (30")	varies
Primrose	*Primula* spp.	varies	varies
Bloodroot	*Sanguinaria canadensis*	15 cm (6")	15 cm (6")
Trillium	*Trillium ovatum*	10–15 cm (4–6")	varies
Globeflower	*Trollius* spp.	40–90 cm (16–36")	25–50 cm (10–20")
Periwinkle	*Vinca minor*	10–15 cm (4–6")	30–45 cm (12–18")
Canada Violet	*Viola canadensis*	25–40 cm (10–16")	25–40 cm (10–16")

FOLIAGE COLOUR	FLOWER COLOUR	COMMENTS
purple green	blue	partial to dense shade
green	white	partial shade
green	white	partial to dense shade
green	wide variety	partial shade
green	blue and cream	partial shade
green	pink	partial shade
green	rosy pink	partial to dense shade
green	blue, purple, white	partial shade
green	purplish blue	partial shade
green	white	partial to dense shade
green	white	partial shade
green	wide variety	partial shade
green	pink, white	partial shade
blue green	inconspicuous	partial shade
green	blue	partial shade
green	wide variety	partial shade
varies	lavender, white	partial to dense shade
green	white to blue	partial shade
green, silver	pink, purple, white	partial to dense shade
green	yellow, gold	partial shade (wilts in full sun)
green	orange	partial shade
green	yellow	partial shade, invasive, mat forming
green	none	partial to dense shade
green	blue	partial to dense shade
green	blue	partial shade
green	pink, blue, purple, white	partial shade
green	pink, blue, white	partial shade
green	white with green	partial shade
green	wide variety	partial shade
green	white	partial to dense shade
green	white	partial to dense shade
green	orange, yellow	partial shade
variegated green	blue, purple, white	partial to dense shade, ground cover
green	white	partial shade

CHAPTER
12

THE COLOUR GARDEN

"Earth laughs in flowers"

–Ralph Waldo Emerson

Gardening is the most colourful of the performing arts—each season brings a new cast of characters in richly coloured costumes. It is frequently this tapestry of costumes that stirs the gardener's creativity. For some gardeners it finds expression in flamboyant colours that excite. Others find it in calm pastels that soothe. Whether your tastes run to the riotous or the subtle, colour is among your most powerful creative tools.

WORKING WITH COLOUR

The best colour gardens begin with a mind to extending indoor living space to the outdoors. This connection between the interior and exterior will be reinforced if you select a common colour range. Usually, the colour scheme is dictated by the exterior of your house. But if you plan on cutting lavish bouquets to display indoors, perhaps your choices should include colours that complement your interior colour scheme.

The place to turn to for effective colour combinations is the colour wheel, a device showing the basic interrelationships of colours. Any three adjoining colours on the colour wheel are *analogous*. Plants with analogous colours include, for example, crimson red salvia, fiery orange day lilies and brilliant orange calendula. This combination is very appealing in a setting near a house with a pale yellow or brown exterior.

Colours opposite each other

Used effectively, colour evokes a broad range of moods and adds vitality to your garden design.

Red, red-orange and orange annual nemesias illustrate an analogous colour scheme.

Complementary orange marigolds and violet-blue lobelias provide a powerful exhibition of colour.

are *complementary*. Yellow complements violet, orange complements blue, red complements green and so on. To imagine the effect of complementary colours in your garden, picture yellow marigolds next to deep violet ageratum. This combination is very effective adjacent to homes with predominantly soft white or blue exteriors. When using the colour wheel to select combinations, remember that flowers are seldom as pure in colour as the examples depicted on the wheel. Typically, they are shades and tints of pure colours.

Your search for ideal colours to complement your home may also end with a *monochromatic* scheme—variations upon a single colour. For example, against a blue-grey house a flower bed in various nuances of pink—from blushing to magenta—is particularly attractive. Pastel shades are also very effective for designing monochromatic colour schemes.

DESIGNING COLOUR GARDENS

Whatever colour scheme you choose for your garden, a plan will help you integrate colour into the basic design elements of balance, rhythm and proportion to create artful arrangements.

Balance

If your colour garden design includes many colours, ensure they are evenly distributed. Too much of a particular colour on one side of the flower bed, for instance, draws the viewer's eye away from the total effect. Keep in mind that odd-numbered groupings of three, five and seven (depending on the mature plant size) of the same flower colour will create more visual impact than even-numbered groupings. Remember, too, that certain colours in combination draw visual strength and emphasis from one another. For example, bright pink flowers appear more vivid beside white companions, and those same white companions can act as neutral peacemakers between colours like hot pink and bright orange.

Besides their colourful attributes, flowers also come in an endless variety of textures. Some plants appear delicate and airy; others appear solid and strong. When designing, be conscious of the need to also achieve a balanced distribution of these textural qualities.

Rhythm

Within a well-balanced design there is still a need for rhythm—the repetition of colour that supplies a sense of continuity from one plant grouping to another. The varying heights of plants and your strategy for incorporating them into the garden will have a profound effect upon the sense of rhythm you seek to establish. Strive for natural-looking arrangements that are not too rigidly tiered with colour groupings too strictly defined. Instead, allow currents of colour to drift in and around one other, creating a soft harmonious effect. For

Blooming in unison, the complementary colours and forms of yellow coreopsis and purple verbenas compose a delightful summer picture.

Various tints and shades of one colour drift together in this wall tapestry illustrating a monochromatic colour scheme.

example, it is typical when designing borders against hedges or fences to place taller species in the background, but to strengthen the effect and create an appealing sense of rhythm, group tall flowers of one colour together rather than planting them in a straight row. Then plant a variety of flowers of medium height to hide any unsightly foliage on the taller companions. Continue this staged descent, but remember to group plants so that a pleasant undulating rhythm of colour is created rather than a series of sharply defined steps. If you are designing an island flower bed (one that is viewed from all sides), the arrangement of heights and colours changes. Flowers now descend from a centre of tall varieties toward lower-growing species.

Proportion

Proportion is also an important element of successful colour garden design. Even the most expertly planned colour garden will be ineffective if it is not proportionate to its surroundings. A very tiny bed, even when it's brimming with the brightest of blooms, can easily go unnoticed near a large two-storey house.

SELECTING A SITE

The first step in designing a colour garden is to determine the vantage point from which it will most often be viewed. If, for example, you spend a great deal of time relaxing on the patio, locate the garden where it can be most appreciated. And don't forget the possibility of making colour visible from within your house. Floral pastels, for instance, add a soothing touch to the vistas from a dining room window. A few brightly coloured blooms may offer a hearty welcome by the front door.

For the largest scope of plant material to design with, select a site that receives a least six hours of sunlight per day. Well-drained organically rich soil and a location away from large trees are also desirable. But even if conditions are not ideal, don't despair. Alberta gardeners can choose from virtually hundreds of cheerful annuals and colourful perennials to suit almost any location.

MONOCHROMATIC GARDENS
Tranquil Blues Throughout the Season

In garden design, drifts of azure flowers perform optical magic because blue tends to recede, melting into shadows and merging with the sky. As a consequence, predominantly blue gardens appear much larger than they are. Blue also evokes feelings of tranquillity, making it ideal for quiet garden retreats.

In the spring perennial garden, the squill (*Scilla sibirica* 'Spring Beauty'), grape hyacinth (*Muscari armeniacum* 'Blue Spike'), puschkinia (*Puschkinia scilloides* var. *libanotica*) and glory-of-the-snow (*Chionodoxa lucilliae*) offer delightful shades and tints of blue. Plant these with the early spring iris (*Iris*

White and silver plants act as neutral peacemakers between fiery colour combinations.

The sky-blue colour of these tall delphiniums unifies this informal garden.

Transform a neglected back alley into a tapestry of summer colour. California poppies, daisies, lupins and speedwells are companions to an informal planting of delphiniums.

reticulata) in the rock garden or at the edge your flower border. The nostalgic forget-me-not (*Myosotis sylvatica* 'Victoria Blue') is also an ideal spring bloomer. It disguises itself as a perennial but is actually a biennial and is perfect for naturalizing in the dappled shade of trees.

Incorporate the later blooming bearded iris (*Iris* x *germanica*) to mark the procession of spring into summer. Blue iris connoisseurs will enjoy many examples of the hybridizer's art such as the captivating cultivars 'Honky Tonk Blues,' 'Babbling Brook,' 'Memphis Blues' and 'Sapphire Hills.'

Meld earth and sky together with a group of tall blue delphiniums (*Delphinium elatum* 'Blue Jay') at the back of the summer perennial garden. Beneath them create rolling waves of cool blues with perennial cornflower (*Centaurea montana*), bellflower (*Campanula* spp.), perennial aster (*Erigeron speciosus* var. *macranthus*) and globe thistle (*Echinops ritro*). A bolder statement can be made with the tall blue spikes of Veronica (*Veronica* x 'Sunny Border Blue'), which is also an excellent cutting flower. Use masses of low-growing dragonhead (*Dracocephalum grandiflorum*) to provide a ribbon of colour at the front. The white flowers of snow-in-summer (*Cerastium tomentosum*) are an ideal low-growing companion.

Shades of blue abound in annual flowers that are equally suited to both borders and con-

This enchanting blue garden offers a gentle rhythm of colour and form to comfort the spirit. Blues can also be woven into existing gardens to complement blushing pinks and clear white companions.

tainers. Try the profusely blooming petunia 'Blue Daddy' (*Petunia* x *hybrida* 'Blue Daddy') or the China aster 'Milady Blue' (*Callistephus chinensis* 'Milady Blue') for mass plantings in sunny borders. The spreading verbena 'Blue Lagoon' (*Verbena* x *hybrida* 'Blue Lagoon') is at home in front of the erect spikes of the salvia 'Victoria Blue' (*Salvia farinacea* 'Victoria Blue'). Consider pairing ageratum (*Ageratum houstonianum* 'Blue Blazer') and bicoloured pansies (*Viola* x *wittrockiana* 'Silver Wings') near annual candytuft (*Iberis* spp.). Arbors, trellises or fences can be smothered in the trumpet-shaped blooms of morning glory (*Ipomoea* 'Heavenly Blue') or the perfumed flowers of tall sweet peas (*Lathyrus odoratus* 'Spencer Mix').

Bring the tranquillity of the blue garden onto decks and patios with containers brim-

In partial shade, the dainty perennial bellflower spills blue colour over a sidewalk.

Sun is the elixir of life for these annual lavender-blue marguerites. For an attractive display, try them next to dark blue lobelia.

ming with blue pansies (*Viola* x *wittrockiana* 'Silver Wings') and ageratum (*Ageratum houstonianum* 'Blue Blazer'), with lobelia (*Lobelia erinus* 'Crystal Palace') cascading over the side. For partial shade conditions, consider browallia (*Browallia speciosa* 'Marine Bells'), which blooms in glorious masses.

Designers of blue gardens learn quickly that pure blue flowers are rare and that the many shades and tints of blue do not always combine harmoniously. There are, however, some painterly qualities of other colours that can help unify the blue garden composition. Silver- and grey-foliaged plants such as lavender cotton (*Santolina chamaecyparissus*) and lamb's ears (*Stachys byzantina*), for example, should be incorporated into the design as peacemakers between the quarreling hues of soft sky blue and deep violet blue.

Astilbe offers plumes of finely spun pink flowers and dark green foliage. Ideal for organically rich soil and less-than-perfect light.

Romantic Pinks
Throughout the Season

A warm welcoming garden composed of pastel blushing pinks is a favourite of many Alberta gardeners. Pinks bring the world of romance to the garden with the flirtatious blushes and captivating charms of shrubs and plants like flowering plums, hybrid lilies and gladioli in costumes ranging from cotton candy pink to magenta.

Spring comes calling in the pink garden with the arrival of the early blooms of shrubs, trees, crocuses and tulips, which can be devel-

Pink garden fanciers can enjoy the luscious blooms of hybrid tea roses. Plant in sunny locations and provide winter protection.

oped into arresting combinations. Among the pink flowering shrubs ideal for Alberta gardens are the Russian almond (*Prunus tenella*), double flowering plum (*Prunus triloba* 'Multiplex'), Nanking cherry (*Prunus tomentosa*) and purple leaved sandcherry (*Prunus* x *cistena*). For attractive companion plantings consider the range of pink Asiatic lilies (*Lilium* spp.) such as the cultivars 'Crete,' 'Malta,' 'Corsica' or 'Polka Dot.' Among flowering trees suitable for the pink garden are the rosybloom crabapples (*Malus* x *astringens*). From the deep rose blooms of the cultivar 'Almey' to the double pink flowers of 'Kelsey,' these lovely spring flowering trees can be underplanted with the pink pansy 'Imperial Frosty Rose' (*Viola* x *wittrockiana* 'Imperial Frosty Rose') or the peach-blossomed tulip (*Tulipa* 'Peach Blossom'), the size of brandy snifters.

With the flowering of a wide variety of perennials and annuals, the romance with the pink garden deepens throughout the summer months. No pink garden design should omit the possibility of hardy shrub roses (*Rosa* spp.). The pastel 'Prairie Dawn,' the deep pink 'David Thompson' and the delightful 'Jens Munk' will provide not just elegant form and sweet scent but an entire framework within which other summer flowering pinks take their place. The deep orchid pink blooms of the vigorous 'John Davies' are quite suitable for growing next to an arbor or beside a tall fence. For smaller gardens, the low-growing 'Martin Frobisher' will create a floral carpet of mauve-pink blooms.

Weave into a framework of roses a selection of perennials and annuals. Consider the clematis 'Bee's Jubilee' (*Clematis* 'Bee's Jubilee') cascading delicate mauve-pink blooms over a trellis in a formally styled garden in which a garden obelisk covered with pink sweet peas makes an attractive focal point. For the back of a flower border, try the pink delphinium

Clematis, the queen of climbers, bears a profusion of delightful flowers in an endless assortment of colours. This clematis drapes pink bell-shaped flowers over a trellis.

Dahlias offer endless summer colour to the garden. This delicious pink cultivar is easily the star of the pink flower border.

Ground-hugging pink rockcress is ideal for sunny rock gardens. These brightly coloured flowers prefer full sun and well-drained soil.

(*Delphinium elatum* 'Raspberry Rose') beside the scented bee balm (*Monarda didyma* 'Croftway Pink'). The annual lavatera (*Lavatera trimestris* 'Silver Cup') offers glistening pink blooms in the background and looks especially effective with the daisylike flowers of the annual cosmos (*Cosmos bipannatus*). For selections of medium height, there are pink poppies (*Papaver* spp.), peonies (*Paeonia lactiflora* 'Sarah Bernhardt'), garden mums (*Chrysanthemum* x *morifolium* 'Morden Candy'), daylilies (*Hemerocallis* 'Catherine Woodbury') and pink bleeding hearts (*Dicentra spectablis*). Border your pink flower bed with petunias (*Petunia* x *hybrida* 'Pink Daddy'), clarkia (*Clarkia elegans* 'Royal Banquet Mix'), the deep rose-pink crepis (*Crepis rubra* 'Rosea') or the sweetly scented candytuft (*Iberis umbellata*), which bears clusters of light pink, mauve, magenta and salmon pink flowers.

To create the most arresting pink garden, the wise gardener will test the effect of pink against the colours of existing structures and plants. The pink garden, for example, is particularly stunning in front of blue or grey foliage, a white picket fence or a grey stone wall, but it seems to argue with red-orange bricks or red-brown decks or fences.

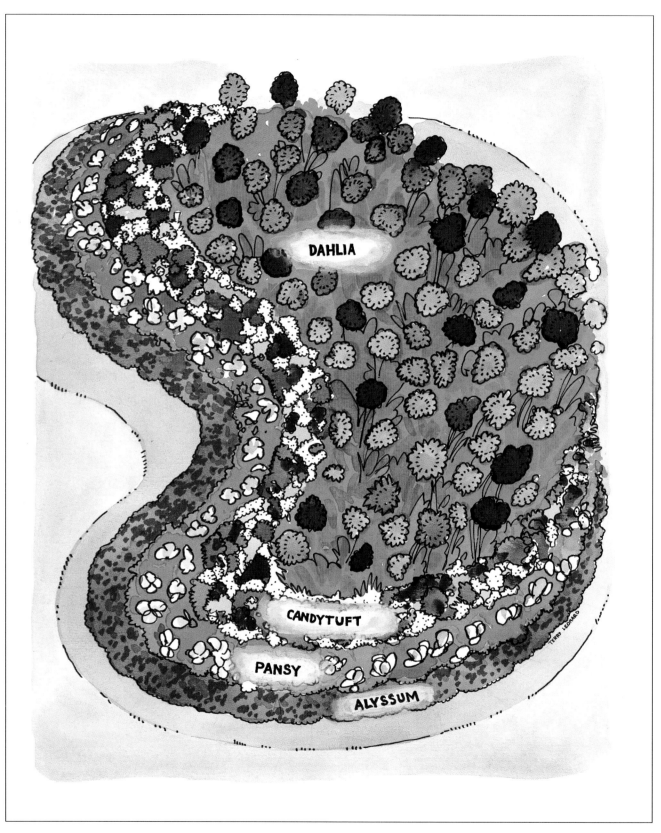

Colour garden fanciers will enjoy this island bed abounding in romantic blooms in vibrant shades of pink. From scented alyssum through cheerful pansies and delicate candytuft to the star feature—the much-loved dahlias—this entire island bed builds toward a stunning crescendo.

Timeless Whites Throughout the Season

When legendary British garden designer Gertrude Jekyll wrote that the purpose of a garden "is to give happiness and repose of mind," she may have been thinking of the timeless appeal of the white garden. Nothing adds old-fashioned charm and subtle beauty to the garden like white-flowering plants.

Spring arrives in the aristocratic white garden with the unhurried unfolding of elegant white tulips (*Tulipa* spp.). Consider the cultivar 'Purissima' for large long-lasting blooms or the popular 'Diana' with fragrant pure white flowers. The fully double tulip 'Mount Tacoma,' with ruffled peonylike petals, is also captivating. Consider as well the graceful white bleeding heart (*Dicentra spectabilis* 'Alba'), whose arching branches bear pure white heart-shaped flowers that hang like charms on a bracelet, making them as irresistible as cut flowers. For an attractive white companion, consider the columbine 'Snow Queen' (*Aquilegia* 'Snow Queen') with its blooms like old-fashioned bonnets.

By summer, the white garden is at its peak—dazzling in sunlight and lustrous in moonlight, the ideal setting for those whose tastes run to the romantic. But even though the garden is composed of a single colour, it must still rely on the elements of balance and rhythm. Here, however, the character of the garden is expressed in terms of form—in the even distribution of distinctive shapes. The effect you should

Lilies offer understated elegance to the white garden. Plant these stunning perennials in full sun and well-drained soil.

With some persistence, Alberta gardeners may enjoy the tranquil white blooms of Japanese irises. Pay close attention to their cultural requirements.

attempt to achieve is not unlike that of fine lace, where pattern, not colour, establishes the mood.

For edging a sunny white perennial border, consider perennial candytuft (*Iberis sempervirens* 'Snowflake'), mother-of-thyme (*Thymus serpyllum* 'Album') or snow-in-summer (*Cerastium tomentosum*), each of which will provide a gently scalloped effect. Weave the middle ground of the border with white shasta daisies (*Chrysanthemum x superbum*) leaning shoulder to shoulder but punctuated occasionally by the erect spikes of gayfeather (*Liatris spicata* 'Alba'). Both are wonderful cut flowers. The peachleaf bellflower (*Campanula persicifolia* 'Snow drift'), aptly named, waves delicately flared white bells, also making a showy display in the middle of the border. These perennials are very effective in front of the tall white spires of delphinium (*Delphinium elatum* 'Galahad').

One of the most adaptable low-maintenance white-flowering perennials is the daylily (*Hemerocallis* spp.). "Beautiful for a day" is the translation of their Greek genus name. Their lovely funnel-shaped flowers bloom day by day, one after another and are ideal for naturalizing in moist areas. In sun or partial shade locations, consider the cultivar 'Ski Jump' for its ruffled scented flowers.

A white garden doesn't seem quite proper without the ruffled petals of a peony (*Paeonia* spp.), which is a perfect single accent plant to place, for instance, at the end of a pathway. This

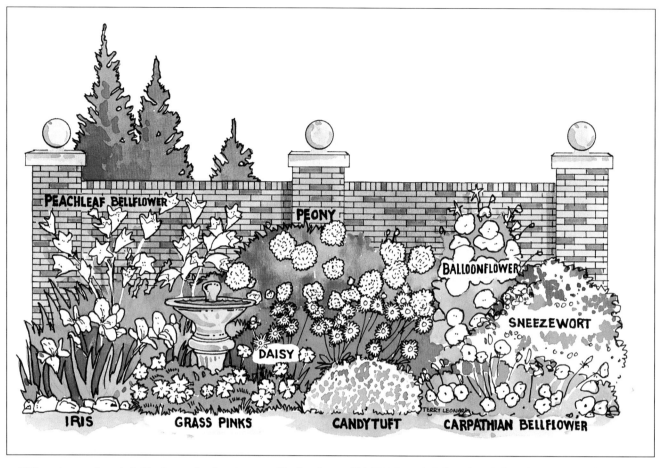

White gardens are always in fashion because they impart a sense of timeless elegance. This Victorian-style design softens the imposing symmetry of the brick wall with informal planting arrangements and a variety of delicate shapes and textures.

long-lived perennial will require staking or wire hoops to support its heavy blooms. Don't overlook the cultivar 'Festiva Maxima' with its deliciously fragrant double white blooms.

For connoisseurs of tranquil white annuals, the list of available selections is extensive.

For an elegant display, use the annual snapdragon (*Antirrhinum majus* 'Tahiti White') *en masse*. Other lovely additions to the white summer garden include zonal geraniums (*Pelargonium* x *hortorum* 'Alba'), petunias (*Petunia* x *hybrida* 'White Cascade'), pansies (*Viola* x *wittrockiana* 'Crystal Bowl White'), alyssum (*Lobularia maritima* 'Carpet of Snow'), lobelia

Night gardens can enjoy an arbor of frosty white clematis. To offer appropriate growing conditions, keep the roots cool with a low-growing companion.

(*Lobelia erinus* 'White Lady') and the glistening white flowers of lavatera (*Lavatera trimestris* 'Mont Blanc').

Besides illuminating the garden by night, white flowers offer among the sweetest of fragrances. After a hard day at work nothing is quite as enticing as a warm summer night spent on your patio or deck enjoying crowded containers of nicotiana (*Nicotiana* 'White Bedder') and evening-scented stocks (*Matthiola longipetala*). To add a touch of elegance to your evening setting, consider installing lamps on patio posts or poles. These create interesting shadows and illuminate the area for entertaining.

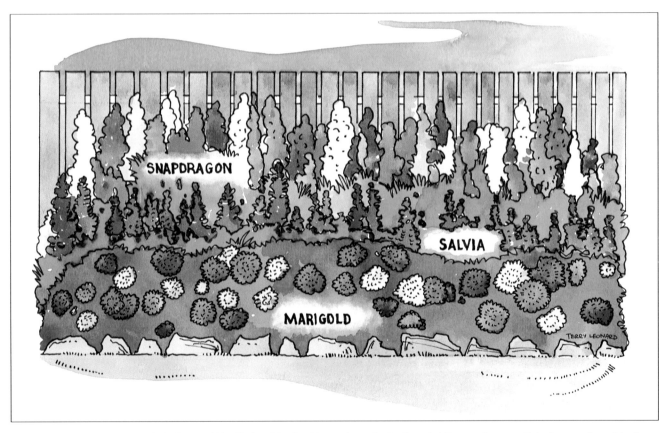

Enliven your garden with a festival of colours. Within this riot of dazzling blooms, the graduating flower heights suggest a sense of intention as well as celebration.

POLYCHROMATIC GARDENS

Calypso Magic Throughout the Season

Colour in the garden is the medium of mood, and moods are highly personal affairs. If the tranquil, romantic or subtle effects of blue, pink and white are not to your taste, then create a carnival of colour with vibrant reds, oranges and yellows. Create a calypso garden that shouts out for life and activity, for music and dance.

Announce a festival of colour in the spring garden with a profusion of yellow, red and orange tulips (*Tulipa* spp.). Try the double yellow cultivar 'Hytuna,' the glorious apricot-orange 'Orange Emperor' or the intense red-blooming 'Parade.' But take cues from nature's own artful colour combinations and under-plant them with a blue carpet of grape hyacinths (*Muscari* spp.) to harmonize the planting with the rest of garden. Another early blooming vivid perennial to consider is the globeflower (*Trollius* spp.). Its large but-tercuplike flowers, in both yellow and orange, make it

an attractive addition to the spring display. These cheerful companions make great cut flowers.

Continue the revelry into the summer with many shades of red, orange and yellow daylilies (*Hemerocallis* spp.). Although each flower lasts but a day, once estab-lished, they will provide stunning blooms for several weeks. Daylilies flourish in both sun and partial shade. The cultivar 'Hyperion,' with its huge lemon yellow flowers, is a colourful companion next to the bold red flowers of the Maltese cross (*Lychnis chalcedonica*). Sun-worshipping heliopsis (*Heliopsis scabra* 'Excelsa'), cone-flower (*Rudbeckia laciniata* 'Golden Glow'), fernleaf yarrow (*Achillea filipendulina* 'Gold Plate') and a group-ing of dramatic Asiatic lilies such as *Lilium* 'Connecticut King' or 'Rhodos' make a striking display against a white, brown or cedar fence or home. Consider the rich canary-yellow flowers of 'Yellow Blaze' and the cherry red blooms of 'Moulin Rouge.' Group these with the fiery orange 'Impact' and you have as riotous a combi-nation as nature allows.

Annuals abound in calypso colours. These zinnias provide bold red flowers—perfect for cutting.

Don't overlook the potential of golden-coloured hardy shrubs to contribute colour, form and texture to your calypso-coloured garden. The upright spreading golden elder (*Sambucus racemosa* 'Plumosa Aurea') or the neat moundlike gold twig dogwood (*Cornus sericea* 'Flaviramea') will both bring variety of form to the calypso garden. Smaller shrubs to consider include 'Gold Flame' spirea (*Spiraea* x *bumalda* 'Gold Flame'), golden broom (*Cytisus ratisbonensis*) and Dyer's Greenwood (*Genista tinctoria*). For extending flowering shrubs consider the hardy potentilla (*Potentilla fruticosa*) available in a variety of warm colours. Try the cultivar 'Goldfinger' (*Potentilla fruticosa* 'Goldfinger') for bright yellow flowers or the 'Red Ace' (*Potentilla fruticosa* 'Red Ace') for reddish flowers.

Extend your celebration of colour well into the late summer with the plumes of goldenrod (*Solidago* spp.). Garden mums (*Chrysanthemum* spp.), another late-flowering favourite, have daisylike flowers with aromatic leaves. Try 'Morden Canary' for double yellow blooms or 'Morden Delight' for double reds. A thickly planted bed of garden mums will also provide fresh flowers for cutting. Considered marginally hardy in areas of little snow cover and fluctuating temperatures, these cultivars will require a little diligence.

Create a salsa-hot display with fiery-coloured hybrid lilies. Ideal for full sun and well-drained soil.

THE CONTAINER GARDEN

Gardeners don't need large landscapes for the expression of their talents. What counts is the artful arrangement of plants and structures, and this quality is equally at home on a balcony, deck, patio or even in a single window box. Any of these can become an oasis of colour and fragrance.

Like many other kinds of gardens, container gardens owe their origins to the ancient Greeks. In ancient Greece, women planted quick-growing seeds of lettuce, fennel, wheat or barley in pots for the festival of Adonis. This ritual represented the reproductive life-cycle of all growing things and eventually came to symbolize impermanence and the fleeting pleasures of life.

Ancient gardeners soon began using containers to adorn their homes. Pots of orange trees and oleander decorated marble colonnades, and smaller receptacles of flowers provided contrast along courtyard walls. From the Hanging Gardens of Babylonia to the courtyard gardens of Europe, the practice of raising plants in containers gave pleasure and satisfied the need to cultivate and tend.

Today, Alberta gardeners can employ this timeless garden style to create in miniature any of the nine specialty gardens described in this book. Think of your outdoor living space as a garden room, one with a floor, walls and a ceiling. Use the walls to support vertical gardens, the ceiling to suspend overhead trailing plants and the floor to create a carpet of colour. The mobility of containers will allow you to rearrange the scene to suit your changing needs.

Container gardening at its best. These movable treasures offer cheerful summer colours and sweet perfumes.

An arbor planting cascading with colour enlivens this garden entrance.

Pink geraniums, white petunias and lobelias adorn these decorative earthen pots. Ideal for sunny entrances.

SELECTING A CONTAINER

An incredibly wide range of containers is available for the imaginative gardener. Garden centres and boutiques offer many shapes and sizes—from whimsical clay animals to wonderful reproductions of ancient urns. If your plan calls for unique containers—anything from salvaged tea kettles to antique wooden boxes—take care to provide adequate drainage. Whatever containers you select, make sure they are sufficiently large and deep for plants to develop healthy root structures. At the end of the season, clean your containers thoroughly to avoid overwintering disease organisms.

PLANTING CONSIDERATIONS

A suitable soil is essential for healthy container flowers. Ideally, it should contain equal parts of loam, perlite or vermiculite and organic matter such as peat moss or compost. Because garden soil often contains annoying weed seeds and insects, opt for commercial potting mixes if your budget allows it. They are easy to use, readily available and provide the necessary aeration for strong root growth.

Plants grown in containers demand closer attention than the same plants grown in a flower bed. Because roots are somewhat constricted in containers, you must compensate by watering and feeding more frequently. Some gardeners prefer to fertilize with a weak nutrient solution every week or so during the summer. Others prefer using time-release fertilizers. Whatever you decide, check the manufacturer's recommendation for correct rates of application.

To get a head start on the season, plant containers a week or so before the last frost, but bring them indoors each evening to protect them from the chilly nights.

DESIGNING WITH CONTAINERS

Container gardens are telescoped views of gardens planted in the ground, so the same principles of design apply. The difference is that the limited amount of available space can make incorporating complex designs difficult, especially in smaller containers. A modest container brimming with seven or eight contrasting colours may, for instance, look less like calypso magic and more like unintentional chaos. The key to designing container plantings is, therefore, simplicity. While heeding the principles of bal-

Steps of colourful geraniums complement this jardiniere planting.

ance, rhythm and proportion, it is best not to mix more than two or three colours, textures or forms within a single small container.

When selecting plants for containers, look closely at the special qualities of each plant and how it will interact with the decorating scheme of your outdoor room. Some plants are tall and will provide vertical accent. Others are tiny and only suitable for cascading blooms down the sides. Whatever your eventual plant selections, strive to create containers that harmonize with their surroundings. A spring container can be as simple as terra cotta pots of dainty jewel-toned primroses (*Primula* spp.) beside your favourite lawn chair or decorating the front step. A discarded canner and a single water lily (*Nymphaea* spp.) can suggest a water garden. Old whiskey barrel sections crowded with nasturtiums (*Tropaeolum majus*) and calendula (*Calendula officinalis*) can double as summer cutting gardens and scented gardens. Large earthenware pots of hybrid roses (*Rosa* spp.) can mimic miniature rose gardens. The cheerful colours of tuberous begonias (*Begonia* x tuberhybrida) can turn into containerized shade gardens. The possibilities are only as limited as your own curiosity and imagination.

THE BLUE GARDEN

COMMON NAME	BOTANICAL NAME	HEIGHT
Annuals		
Ageratum	*Ageratum houstonianum* 'Blue Blazer'	15–20 cm (6–8")
Swan River Daisy	*Brachycome iberidifolia*	30 cm (12")
Browallia	*Browallia speciosa* 'Marine Bells'	25–35 cm (10–14")
China Aster	*Callistephus chinensis* 'Milady Blue'	25 cm (10")
Annual Candytuft	*Iberis* spp.	10–15 cm (4–6")
Morning Glory	*Ipomoea* 'Heavenly Blue'	2–3 M (7–10')
Dwarf Sweet Pea	*Lathyrus odoratus* 'Knee-Hi'	15–30 cm (6–12")
Tall Sweet Pea	*Lathyrus odoratus* 'Spencer Mix'	3 M (10')
Lobelia	*Lobelia erinus* 'Crystal Palace'	10–15 cm (4–6")
Sweet Alyssum	*Lobularia maritima* 'Royal Carpet'	5–10 cm (2–4")
Baby-Blue-Eyes	*Nemophila menziesii*	8–12 cm (3–5")
Petunia	*Petunia* x *hybrida* 'Blue Daddy'	15–30 cm (6–12")
Salvia	*Salvia farinacea* 'Victoria Blue'	45–50 cm (18–20")
Verbena	*Verbena* x *hybrida* 'Blue Lagoon'	20 cm (8")
Pansy	*Viola* x *wittrockiana* 'Silver Wings'	10–15 cm (4–6")
Perennials		
Monkshood	*Aconitum napellus*	1–1.5 M (3–5')
Carpet Bugleweed	*Ajuga reptans* 'Catlin's Giant'	10 cm (4")
Italian Bugloss	*Anchusa azurea* 'Morning Glory'	1–1.3 M (3–4')
Columbine	*Aquilegia alpina*	30–60 cm (12–24")
Carpathian Bellflower	*Campanula carpatica*	20 cm (8")
Creeping Bellflower	*Campanula cochleariifolia*	8–10 cm (3–4")
Clustered Bellflower	*Campanula glomerata*	60 cm (24")
Cornflower	*Centaurea montana*	60 cm (24")
Delphinium	*Delphinium elatum* 'Blue Jay'	1.3–2 M (4–7')
Dragonhead	*Dracocephalum grandiflorum*	20 cm (8")
Globe Thistle	*Echinops ritro*	1 M (3')
Perennial Aster	*Erigeron speciosus* var. *macranthus*	30–60 cm (12–24")
Sea Holly	*Eryngium planum* 'Azureum'	60–90 cm (24–36")
Mountain Gentian	*Gentiana acaulis*	10 cm (4")
Caucasian Cranesbill	*Geranium* x 'Johnson's Blue'	45–50 cm (18–20")
Sea Lavender	*Limonium latifolium*	60–75 cm (24–30")
Perennial Flax	*Linum perenne*	25–30 cm (10–12")
Lupin	*Lupinus* spp.	60 cm–1.5 M (2–5')
Himalayan Blue Poppy	*Meconopsis betonicifolia*	90 cm (36")
Virginia Bluebells	*Mertensia virginica*	60 cm (24")
Forget-Me-Not	*Myosotis sylvatica* 'Victoria Blue'	30 cm (12")
Purple Haze Bearded Tongue	*Penstemon fruticosus* 'Purple Haze'	30–90 cm (12–36")
Creeping Phlox	*Phlox subulata* 'Emerald Blue'	10–15 cm (4–6")
Balloonflower	*Platycodon grandiflorum* 'Misato'	20–30 cm (8–12")
Jacob's Ladder	*Polemonium caeruleum*	60 cm (24")
Thyme	*Thymus praecox* 'Purple Carpet'	5 cm (2")
Veronica	*Veronica* x 'Sunny Border Blue'	45–60 cm (18–24")

144

SPREAD	COMMENTS
15–20 cm (6–8")	good in containers
25 cm (10")	excellent in hanging baskets
varies	good in containers
10–15 cm (4–6")	ideal in beds and containers
10–15 cm (4–6")	ideal in fronts of borders
varies	lovely hanging plant, especially against trelliswork
15–30 cm (6–12")	scented blooms, ideal in containers
5–15 cm (2–6")	scented, excellent cut flower
varies	good for edging, masses of colour
25 cm (10")	scented, compact
varies	good in containers
15–30 cm (6–12")	good in fronts of borders and containers
varies	extended flowering on thin flower spikes
20 cm (8")	excellent in hanging baskets
varies	bicolour, excellent in borders and containers
30–45 cm (12–18")	good in backs of borders
30–45 cm (12–18")	excellent for edging
30–45 cm (12–18")	intense blooms borne on tall stems
30–60 cm (12–24")	ideal in rockeries
varies	neat mound of bell-shaped blooms
varies	good for edging or rockeries
varies	showy en masse, aggressive
30–40 cm (12–16")	large thistlelike blooms
25–50 cm (10–20")	tall spires of bloom
varies	attractive clear blue blooms
1 M (3')	dramatic thistlelike blooms, excellent cut flower
30–60 cm (12–24")	daisylike blooms with yellow centres
varies	good in fresh and dried arrangements
30 cm (12")	trumpet-shaped blooms, useful in rockeries
varies	lovely in sunny borders, profuse bloomer
60 cm (24")	excellent in borders or as cut flower
30–45 cm (12–18")	good for naturalizing in dry sandy soil
60 cm–1.5 M (2–5')	excellent cut flower
30 cm (12")	crisp sky-blue blooms with yellow stamens
30–45 cm (12–18")	bell-shaped blooms in nodding clusters
varies	true biennial, mounds of light blue blooms
varies	ideal in rockeries and fronts of borders
30–45 cm (12–18")	excellent in rockeries
25 cm (10")	star-shaped blooms
varies	bell-shaped blooms with fernlike leaves
30 cm (12")	mat-forming, useful in rockeries
30 cm (12")	extended flowering, excellent cut flower

COMMON NAME	BOTANICAL NAME	HEIGHT
The Blue Garden continued		
Bulbs and Others		
Blue Globe Onion	*Allium caeruleum*	60 cm (24")
Glory-of-the-Snow	*Chionodoxa lucilliae*	15 cm (6")
Crocus	*Crocus* 'Queen of the Blues'	10–15 cm (4–6")
Gladioli	*Gladiolus* 'Great River'	1 M (3')
Early Spring Iris	*Iris reticulata*	10–15 cm (4–6")
Bearded Iris	*Iris* x *germanica* 'Babbling Brook'	80–90 cm (32–36")
Bearded Iris	*Iris* x *germanica* 'Honky Tonk Blues'	60–90 cm (24–36")
Bearded Iris	*Iris* x *germanica* 'Memphis Blues'	90 cm (36")
Bearded Iris	*Iris* x *germanica* 'Sapphire Hills'	80–90 cm (32–36")
Grape Hyacinth	*Muscari armeniacum* 'Blue Spike'	10–20 cm (4–8")
Puschkinia	*Puschkinia scilloides* var. *libanotica*	15 cm (6")
Squill	*Scilla sibirica* 'Spring Beauty'	10–15 cm (4–6")

SPREAD	COMMENTS
varies	dramatic globelike flower clusters
varies	spring flowering, starry blue blooms
varies	spring flowering, large blooms
10–15 cm (4–6")	excellent cut flower
varies	spring flowering
varies	large ruffled blooms
varies	lovely ruffled blooms
varies	heavily ruffled blooms
varies	flaired blooms
varies	spring flowering, double blooms
varies	spring flowering, ideal in rockeries
varies	spring flowering, nodding blooms

THE PINK GARDEN

COMMON NAME	BOTANICAL NAME	HEIGHT
Annuals		
Ageratum	*Ageratum houstonianum* 'Fairy Pink'	15–20 cm (6–8")
Snapdragon	*Antirrhinum majus* 'Sonnet Pink'	35–60 cm (14–24")
Swan River Daisy	*Brachycome iberidifolia*	30 cm (12")
China Aster	*Callistephus chinensis* 'Milady Rose'	15–25 cm (6–10")
Clarkia	*Clarkia elegans* 'Royal Banquet Mix'	30–60 cm (12–24")
Cosmos	*Cosmos bipinnatus*	40 cm–1 M (1.5–3')
Crepis	*Crepis rubra* 'Rosea'	30–55 cm (12–22")
Annual Dahlia	*Dahlia pinnata*	15–60 cm (6–24")
Annual Candytuft	*Iberis umbellata*	10–15 cm (4–6")
Sweet Pea	*Lathyrus odoratus*	15 cm–3 M (.5–10')
Lavatera	*Lavatera trimestris* 'Silver Cup'	1 M (3')
Lobelia	*Lobelia erinus* 'Rosamond'	10–15 cm (4–6")
Sweet Alyssum	*Lobularia maritima* 'Wonderland'	5–10 cm (2–4")
Stocks	*Matthiola incana* 'Midget Rose'	20–25 cm (8–10")
Nicotiana	*Nicotiana* 'Domino Picotee'	25–30 cm (10–12")
Ivy Geranium	*Pelargonium peltatum* 'Belladonna'	varies
Martha Washington Geranium	*Pelargonium x domesticum* 'Vavra Josy'	30–45 cm (12–18")
Zonal Geranium	*Pelargonium x hortorum* 'Pink Expectations'	varies
Petunia	*Petunia x hybrida* 'Pink Daddy'	15–30 cm (6–12")
Portulaca	*Portulaca grandiflora* 'Sundial Fuchsia'	5–8 cm (2–3")
Salvia	*Salvia splendens* 'Melba'	20–35 cm (8–14")
Verbena	*Verbena x hybrida* 'Delight'	20–30 cm (8–12")
Pansy	*Viola x wittrockiana* 'Imperial Frosty Rose'	10–15 cm (4–6")
Zinnia	*Zinnia elegans* 'Rose Pinwheel'	12–60 cm (5–24")
Perennials		
Columbine	*Aquilegia* 'Songbird Robin'	30–60 cm (12–24")
Garden Mums	*Chrysanthemum x morifolium* 'Morden Candy'	40–60 cm (16–24")
Delphinium	*Delphinium elatum* 'Raspberry Rose'	60 cm–2 M (2–7')
Maiden Pinks	*Dianthus deltoides* 'Wisely'	15–20 cm (6–8")
Grass Pinks	*Dianthus plumarius* 'Roseus Plenus'	40 cm (16")
Bleeding Heart	*Dicentra spectablis*	90 cm (36")
Daylily	*Hemerocallis* 'Catherine Woodbury'	varies
Gayfeather	*Liatris spicata* 'Floristam Violet'	45–60 cm (18–24")
Lupin	*Lupinus* Hybrids	60 cm–1.5 M (2–5')
Bee Balm	*Monarda didyma* 'Croftway Pink'	60–90 cm (24–36")
Peony	*Paeonia lactiflora* 'Sarah Bernhardt'	varies
Poppy	*Papaver* spp.	30–90 cm (12–36")
Oriental Poppy	*Papaver orientale* 'Pink Lassie'	30–90 cm (12–36")
Beard Tongue	*Penstemon barbatus* 'Elfin Pink'	30–90 cm (12–36")
Garden Phlox	*Phlox paniculata*	60–90 cm (24–36")
Creeping Phlox	*Phlox subulata* 'Laura'	10–15 cm (4–6")
Balloonflower	*Platycodon grandiflorum*	45–60 cm (18–24")
Thyme	*Thymus serpyllum*	varies
Veronica	*Veronica spicata* 'Red Fox'	30–90 cm (12–36")

SPREAD	COMMENTS
15–20 cm (6–8")	good in containers
varies	long-lasting blooms
25 cm (10")	excellent in hanging baskets
15–20 cm (6–8")	good cut flower
30–40 cm (12–16")	spikes of showy blooms
20–40 cm (8–16")	good cut flower
varies	brightly coloured daisylike blooms
30–40 cm (12–16")	excellent cut flower
10–15 cm (4–6")	ideal in fronts of borders or bordering sidewalks
5–15 cm (2–6")	scented, excellent cut flower, dwarf and vine types available
30–40 cm (12–16")	good in backs of borders
varies	excellent in containers
25 cm (10")	compact growth habit
15–20 cm (6–8")	scented, nice cut flower
varies	lovely rose-coloured blooms
varies	excellent in hanging baskets
varies	excellent in containers
varies	good in beds and containers
15–30 cm (6–12")	excellent in beds and containers
30 cm (12")	dense carpet of blooms
varies	excellent in beds and containers
20 cm (8")	excellent in containers
varies	excellent in beds and containers
12–30 cm (5–12")	good cut flower
30–60 cm (12–24")	spurred blooms, graceful foliage
varies	double blooms, nice cut flower
25–50 cm (10–20")	good in backs of borders
30–45 cm (12–18")	mats of carmine blooms
30 cm (12")	scented double blooms
90 cm (36")	drooping chains of soft pink hearts
varies	fragrant orchid-pink blooms
30 cm (12")	excellent cut flower
60 cm–1.5 M (2–5')	tall spires of bloom
60 cm (24")	scented, attracts bees and butterflies
varies	large, ruffled satiny blooms
30–90 cm (12–36")	many shades of pink available
30–90 cm (12–36")	large satiny blooms, hairy foliage
varies	spikes of trumpet-shaped blooms
45–60 cm (18–24")	excellent cut flower
30–45 cm (12–18")	excellent for edging and rockeries
30 cm (12")	star-shaped blooms
varies	mat forming
varies	tall spikes of bloom

COMMON NAME	BOTANICAL NAME	HEIGHT
The Pink Garden continued		
Bulbs and Others		
Tuberous Begonia	*Begonia* x *tuberhybrida* 'Nonstop Pink'	20–45 cm (8–18")
Glory-of-the-Snow	*Chionodoxa lucilliae* 'Rosea'	15 cm (6")
Crocus	*Crocus* 'Ruby Giant'	10–15 cm (4–6")
Gladioli	*Gladiolus* 'Rookie'	1 M (3')
Bearded Iris	*Iris* x *germanica* 'Beverly Sills'	85 cm (34")
Asiatic Lily	*Lilium* 'Corsica'	60 cm (24")
Asiatic Lily	*Lilium* 'Crete'	75 cm (30")
Asiatic Lily	*Lilium* 'Malta'	60–70 cm (24–28")
Asiatic Lily	*Lilium* 'Polka Dot'	60–70 cm (24–28")
Tulip	*Tulipa* 'Peach Blossom'	30 cm (12")
Shrubs and Vines		
Bee's Jubilee Clematis	*Clematis* 'Bee's Jubilee'	4 M (13')
Almey Rosybloom Crabapple	*Malus* x 'Almey'	3–4 M (10–13')
Rosybloom Crabapple	*Malus* x *astringens*	3–5 M (10–16')
Kelsey Rosybloom Crabapple	*Malus* x 'Kelsey'	3–4 M (10–13')
Russian Almond	*Prunus tenella*	75 cm (2.5')
Nanking Cherry	*Prunus tomentosa*	2 M (7')
Double Flowering Plum	*Prunus triloba* 'Multiplex'	2–3 M (7–10')
Purple Leaved Sandcherry	*Prunus* x *cistena*	1–1.5 M (3–5')
Shrub Rose	*Rosa* spp.	varies
David Thompson Rose	*Rosa* x 'David Thompson'	1.2 M (4')
Jens Munk Rose	*Rosa* x 'Jens Munk'	1 M (3')
John Davis Rose	*Rosa* x 'John Davis'	2.2–2.5 M (7.5–8')
Martin Frobisher	*Rosa* x 'Martin Frobisher'	1.5–2 M (5–7')
Prairie Dawn Rose	*Rosa* x 'Prairie Dawn'	2 M (7')

SPREAD	COMMENTS
20–25 cm (8–10")	excellent in containers and shady locations
varies	spring flowering, star-shaped blooms
varies	spring flowering, excellent for naturalizing
10–15 cm (4–6")	excellent cut flower
varies	ruffled blooms
varies	delicate pink blooms
varies	long-lasting blooms
varies	excellent cut flower
varies	excellent cut flower
varies	spring flowering, double blooms
2 M (7')	profuse pink blooms
3–4 M (10–13')	spring flowering
varies	spring flowering
3–4 M (10–13')	spring flowering
75 cm (2.5')	deep pink blooms, suckers, use with discretion
2 M (7')	attractive spring display
2–3 M (7–10')	spectacular spring display
1 M (3')	good contrast
varies	many shades of pink available
1.2 M (4')	dark pink to red blooms
1 M (3')	prolific pink blooms
2–2.5 M (7.5–8')	pink blooms with spicy fragrance
1.5–2 M (5–7')	fragrant pink blooms
2 M (7')	bright pink blooms

THE WHITE GARDEN

COMMON NAME	BOTANICAL NAME	HEIGHT
Annuals		
Ageratum	*Ageratum houstonianum* 'Hawaii White'	15 cm (6")
Snapdragon	*Antirrhinum majus* 'Tahiti White'	15–25 cm (6–10")
Swan River Daisy	*Brachycome iberidifolia*	30 cm (12")
Browallia	*Browallia speciosa* 'Silver Bells'	25–35 cm (10–14")
Calendula	*Calendula officinalis* 'Cream Beauty'	30 cm (12")
China Aster	*Callistephus chinensis* 'Milady White'	25 cm (10")
Cosmos	*Cosmos bipinnatus* 'White Sonata'	40–60 cm (16–24")
Annual Candytuft	*Iberis* 'Giant White Hyacinth'	30 cm (12")
Sweet Pea	*Lathyrus odoratus*	15 cm–3 M (.5–10')
Lavatera	*Lavatera trimestris* 'Mont Blanc'	1 M (3')
Lobelia	*Lobelia erinus* 'White Lady'	10–15 cm (4–6")
Sweet Alyssum	*Lobularia maritima* 'Carpet of Snow'	5–10 cm (2–4")
Stocks	*Matthiola incana* 'Cinderella White'	25 cm (10")
Evening Scented Stocks	*Matthiola longipetala*	45 cm (18")
Nicotiana	*Nicotiana* 'White Bedder'	60 cm (24")
Ivy Geranium	*Pelargonium peltatum* 'Double Lilac White'	varies
Martha Washington Geranium	*Pelargonium* x *domesticum* 'Crystal'	30–45 cm (12–18")
Zonal Geranium	*Pelargonium* x *hortorum* 'Alba'	varies
Petunia	*Petunia* x *hybrida* 'White Cascade'	15–30 cm (6–12")
Portulaca	*Portulaca grandiflora* 'Sundial White'	5–8 cm (2–3")
Salvia	*Salvia splendens* 'Empire White'	25–30 cm (10–12")
Verbena	*Verbena* x *hybrida* 'Novalis White'	20–25 cm (8–10")
Pansy	*Viola* x *wittrockiana* 'Crystal Bowl White'	10–15 cm (4–6")
Zinnia	*Zinnia elegans* 'Star White'	35 cm (14")

SPREAD	COMMENTS
15 cm (6")	good in containers
varies	long-lasting blooms
25 cm (10")	excellent in hanging baskets
varies	good in containers
10–20 cm (4–8")	excellent cut flower
15–20 cm (6–8")	good in borders and containers
20 cm (8")	excellent cut flower
10–15 cm (4–6")	ideal in fronts of borders
5–15 cm (2–6")	both dwarf and vine types available
30–40 cm (12–16")	good in backs of borders, lovely cut flower
varies	excellent in containers
25 cm (10")	ideal in fronts of borders and rockeries
15–20 cm (6–8")	scented, nice cut flower
10 cm (4")	evening-scented blooms
30 cm (12")	scented star-shaped blooms
varies	excellent in containers and hanging baskets
varies	excellent in borders and containers
varies	excellent in borders and containers
15–30 cm (6–12")	excellent in fronts of borders and hanging baskets
30 cm (12")	best in full sun, good in rockeries
varies	dense flowering spikes
20 cm (8")	excellent in hanging baskets, tolerates wind and drought
varies	good in borders and containers
10 cm (4")	extended flowering

COMMON NAME	BOTANICAL NAME	HEIGHT
The White Garden continued		
Perennials		
Sneezewort	*Achillea ptarmica* 'The Pearl'	45–60 cm (18–24")
Columbine	*Aquilegia* 'Snow Queen'	30–60 cm (12–24")
Silver Mound Artemisia	*Artemisia schmidtiana* 'Silver Mound'	30 cm (12")
Carpathian Bellflower	*Campanula carpatica* 'White Clips'	30 cm (12")
Peachleaf Bellflower	*Campanula persicifolia* 'Snowdrift'	60–75 cm (24–30")
Snow-in-Summer	*Cerastium tomentosum*	15 cm (6")
Garden Mums	*Chrysanthemum* x *morifolium* 'Morden Cameo'	40–60 cm (16–24")
Daisy	*Chrysanthemum* x *superbum*	30–90 cm (12–36")
Delphinium	*Delphinium elatum* 'Galahad'	60 cm–2 M (2–7')
Maiden Pinks	*Dianthus deltoides* 'Albus'	15–20 cm (6–8")
Grass Pinks	*Dianthus plumarius* 'Her Majesty'	40 cm (16")
White Bleeding Heart	*Dicentra spectablis* 'Alba'	60–90 cm (24–36")
Daylily	*Hemerocallis* 'Ski Jump'	70 cm (28")
Hosta	*Hosta sieboldiana* 'Bressingham Blue'	30–60 cm (12–24")
Perennial Candytuft	*Iberis sempervirens* 'Snowflake'	30 cm (12")
Gayfeather	*Liatris spicata* 'Alba'	45–60 cm (18–24")
Perennial Flax	*Linum perenne* 'White Diamond'	25–30 cm (10–12")
Peony	*Paeonia lactiflora* 'Festiva Maxima'	1 M (3')
Oriental Poppy	*Papaver orientale*	30–90 cm (12–36")
Garden Phlox	*Phlox paniculata*	60–90 cm (24–36")
Creeping Phlox	*Phlox subulata* 'Snow Queen'	10–15 cm (4–6")
Balloonflower	*Platycodon grandiflorum*	45–60 cm (18–24")
Lavender Cotton	*Santolina chamaecyparissus*	45–60 cm (18–24")
Mother-of-Thyme	*Thymus serpyllum* 'Album'	5–10 cm (2–4")
Veronica	*Veronica spicata* 'Icicle'	30–45 cm (12–18")
Bulbs and Others		
Tuberous Begonia	*Begonia* x *tuberhybrida* 'Billy Langdon'	20–45 cm (8–18")
Glory-of-the-Snow	*Chionodoxa gigantea*	15 cm (6")
Crocus	*Crocus* 'Joan of Arc'	10–15 cm (4–6")
Snowdrop	*Galanthus nivalis*	15–20 cm (6–8")
Gladioli	*Gladiolus* 'White Prosperity'	1 M (3')
Bearded Iris	*Iris* x *germanica* 'Immortality'	60–75 cm (24–30")
Asiatic Lily	*Lilium* 'Roma'	75–90 cm (30–36")
Grape Hyacinth	*Muscari botryoides* 'Album'	10–20 cm (4–8")
Daffodil	*Narcissus* 'Mount Hood'	30–45 cm (12–18")
Puschkinia	*Puschkinia scilloides* var. *libanotica* 'Alba'	15 cm (6")
Squill	*Scilla sibirica* 'Alba'	10–15 cm (4–6")
Tulip	*Tulipa* 'Diana'	35 cm (14")
Tulip	*Tulipa* 'Ivory Floradale'	50–60 cm (20–24")
Tulip	*Tulipa* 'Mount Tacoma'	45 cm (18")
Tulip	*Tulipa* 'Purissima'	50 cm (20")

SPREAD	COMMENTS
45–60 cm (18–24")	masses of tiny blooms, best in full sun
30–60 cm (12–24")	spurred blooms, graceful foliage
45 cm (18")	moundlike form, light silver-grey foliage
30 cm (12")	excellent in fronts of borders and rockeries
varies	very showy en masse
varies	matlike creeping plant, good in rockeries
varies	late bloomer, nice cut flower
varies	best in full sun and well-drained soil
25–50 cm (10–20")	ideal in backs of borders
30–45 cm (12–18")	low spreading mats of tiny blooms
30 cm (12")	scented double blooms
60 cm (24")	arching branches of white hearts
varies	ruffled scented blooms
varies	tall stems, blue-green foliage
30–50 cm (12–20")	compact, mat forming, good for edging and rockeries
30 cm (12")	tall spikes of bloom, attractive cut flower
30–45 cm (12–18")	useful for naturalizing in dry and sandy soil
1 M (3')	fragrant double blooms
30–90 cm (12–36")	large satiny blooms, hairy foliage
45–60 cm (18–24")	scented, excellent cut flower, available by colour
30–45 cm (12–18")	excellent for edging and rockeries
30 cm (12")	star-shaped blooms
25–30 cm (10–12")	moundlike form, silver-grey foliage
20–30 cm (8–12")	scented, mat-forming ground cover
20–25 cm (8–10")	tall spikes, good cut flower
20–25 cm (8–10")	upright form, excellent in containers and shady borders
varies	spring flowering, star-shaped blooms
varies	spring flowering, large blooms
varies	spring flowering, ideal for rockeries
10–15 cm (4–6")	excellent cut flower
varies	heavy bloomer, glistening white blooms
varies	lightly spotted blooms, excellent cut flower
varies	spring flowering, miniature hyacinthlike blooms
varies	spring flowering, large blooms with long trumpets
varies	spring flowering, delicate clusters of bloom
varies	spring flowering, delicate bell-shaped blooms
varies	spring flowering, perfect for borders
varies	spring flowering, perfect for borders
varies	spring flowering, perfect for borders
varies	spring flowering, perfect for borders

THE CALYPSO COLOURED GARDEN

COMMON NAME	BOTANICAL NAME	HEIGHT
Annuals		
Snapdragon	*Antirrhinum majus* 'Carousel'	80 cm (32")
Snapdragon	*Antirrhinum majus* 'Liberty Red'	40–50 cm (16–20")
Calendula	*Calendula officinalis* 'Pacific Beauty'	12–60 cm (5–24")
China Aster	*Callistephus chinensis* 'Milady' series	25 cm (10")
Clarkia	*Clarkia elegans* 'Royal Banquet Mix'	45–60 cm (18–24")
Cosmos	*Cosmos sulphureus* 'Sunny Red'	35–40 cm (14–16")
Sweet Pea	*Lathyrus odoratus* 'Winston Churchill'	25–30 cm (10–12")
Lobelia	*Lobelia erinus* 'Colour Cascade Mixture'	10–15 cm (4–6")
Stocks	*Matthiola incana* 'Cinderella' series	25 cm (10")
Nicotiana	*Nicotiana* 'Starship' series	15 cm–1 M (6–36")
Ladybird Poppy	*Papaver commutatum* 'Ladybird'	30–45 cm (12–18")
Ivy Geranium	*Pelargonium peltatum* 'Summer Showers' series	varies
Martha Washington Geranium	*Pelargonium* x *domesticum* 'Royalty' series	30–45 cm (12–18")
Zonal Geranium	*Pelargonium* x *hortorum* 'Kim'	varies
Petunia	*Petunia* x *hybrida* 'Calypso'	15–30 cm (6–12")
Portulaca	*Portulaca grandiflora* 'Sundance Mix'	5–8 cm (2–3")
Painted Tongue	*Salpiglossis sinuata*	30–45 cm (12–18")
Salvia	*Salvia coccinea* 'Lady in Red'	20–35 cm (8–14")
African Marigold	*Tagetes erecta* 'Excel Primrose'	15–70 cm (6–28")
French Marigold	*Tagetes patula* 'Early Spice Saffron'	10–20 cm (4–8")
Nasturtium	*Tropaeolum majus* 'Whirlybird'	30 cm (12")
Verbena	*Verbena* x *hybrida* 'Peaches and Cream'	20–30 cm (8–12")
Pansy	*Viola* 'Universal Yellow'	10–15 cm (4–6")
Zinnia	*Zinnia erecta* 'Paintbrush'	30–35 cm (12–14")
Zinnia	*Zinnia erecta* 'Scarlet Splendor'	50–60 cm (20–24")
Perennials		
Fernleaf Yarrow	*Achillea filipendulina* 'Gold Plate'	1–1.3 M (3–4')
Common Yarrow	*Achillea millifolium* 'Red Beauty'	45–70 cm (18–28")
Common Yarrow	*Achillea* x 'Summer Pastels' series	45–60 cm (18–24")
Golden Columbine	*Aquilegia chrysantha*	75 cm–1 M (30–36")
Columbine	*Aquilegia* x 'Crimson Star'	60–90 cm (24–36")
Garden Mums	*Chrysanthemum* x *morifolium* 'Morden Canary'	40–60 cm (16–24")
Garden Mums	*Chrysanthemum* x *morifolium* 'Morden Delight'	60 cm (24")
Maiden Pinks	*Dianthus deltoides*	15–20 cm (6–8")
False Heliopsis	*Heliopsis scabra* 'Excelsa'	1 M (3')
Daylily	*Hemerocallis* 'Ginger Whip'	75 cm (30")
Daylily	*Hemerocallis* 'Heart and Soul'	30–35 cm (12–14")
Daylily	*Hemerocallis* 'Hyperion'	1 M (3')
Elephant Ears	*Ligularia* spp.	1–1.3 M (3–4')
Lupin	*Lupinus* spp.	60 cm–1.5 M (2–5')
Maltese Cross	*Lychnis chalcedonica*	1–1.3 M (3–4')

SPREAD	FLOWER COLOUR	COMMENTS
varies	red, orange, yellow	good in backs of borders
varies	red	long-lasting blooms
12–30 cm (5–12")	apricot, orange, yellow	easily grown from seed, good cut flower
15–60 cm (6–24")	red, pink, blue, purple	very showy en masse
30–40 cm (12–16")	red, pink, orange, purple, white	spikes of blooms resembling small roses
15–20 cm (6–8")	red	bright single blooms, good cut flower
5–15 cm (2–6")	red	scented, dwarf variety, good in containers
varies	rose, purple, blue, mauve, white	trailing mixture, good in containers
15–20 cm (6–8")	red, pink, white	spikes of scented blooms
varies	red, pink, green, white	scented, star-shaped blooms
15–25 cm (6–10")	red with dark blotch	very colourful and unique
varies	wide variety	excellent in containers and hanging baskets
varies	pastels, bicolour	excellent in borders and containers
varies	scarlet	very showy en masse
15–30 cm (6–12")	wide variety	many bright colours, good in borders and containers
30 cm (12")	wide variety	forms carpet of colour, good in borders and containers
15–20 cm (6–8")	pink, yellow, bronze, purple	velvet-textured flowers, profuse bloomer
varies	red	heat and drought tolerant, profuse bloomer
varies	yellow	best in full sun, excellent in borders
varies	yellow	best in full sun, excellent in borders
15–60 cm (6–24")	red, salmon, orange, yellow, bronze	scented, good in borders and containers
20 cm (8")	salmon, apricot	drought tolerant, continuous blooms
varies	yellow	good in borders and containers
10–12 cm (4–5")	wide variety	excellent cut flower
12 cm (5")	red	excellent en masse, late summer colour
60 cm (24")	yellow, gold	good summer colour, excellent cut flower
60 cm (24")	deep crimson	drought tolerant, excellent cut flower
60 cm (24")	red, pink, yellow, gold, white	drought tolerant, excellent cut flower
30 cm (12")	yellow	tolerates partial shade
30–60 cm (12–24")	red	bright crimson blooms with white corolla
varies	yellow	late summer colour
30 cm (12")	red	late summer colour
30–45 cm (12–18")	red, pink, white	excellent in rockeries and fronts of borders
1 M (3')	yellow	good for backs of borders, good cut flower
varies	gold	fragrant ruffled blooms
varies	red	fragrant, large, velvety ruffled blooms
1 M (3')	yellow	large fragrant blooms
varies	orange, yellow	good for backs of shady borders
60 cm–1.5 M (2–5')	red, pink, yellow, purple, white	tall spires of colour
30 cm (12")	red, orange	good cut flower

COMMON NAME	BOTANICAL NAME	HEIGHT
The Calypso Coloured Garden continued		
Bee Balm	*Monarda didyma* 'Gardenview Scarlet'	60–90 cm (24–36")
Peony	*Paeonia* 'Red Charm'	1 M (3')
Iceland Poppy	*Papaver nudicaule*	30–40 cm (12–16")
Oriental Poppy	*Papaver orientale* 'Brilliant'	30–90 cm (12–36")
Bearded Tongue	*Penstemon* spp.	30–90 cm (12–36")
Garden Phlox	*Phlox paniculata*	60–90 cm (24–36")
Coneflower	*Rudbeckia laciniata* 'Golden Glow'	1–1.5 M (3–5')
Goldenrod	*Solidago* spp.	1–1.5 M (3–5')
Globeflower	*Trollius* spp.	45–90 cm (18–36")
Bulbs and Others		
Tuberous Begonia	*Begonia* x *tuberhybrida* 'Allan Langdon'	30–45 cm (12–18")
Crocus	*Crocus chrysanthus* 'Zwanenburg Bronze'	10–15 cm (4–6")
Gladioli	*Gladiolus* 'Fire Engine'	1 M (3')
Bearded Iris	*Iris* x *germanica* 'Lemon Mist'	60–75 cm (24–30")
Asiatic Lily	*Lilium* 'Connecticut King'	90 cm (36")
Asiatic Lily	*Lilium* 'Impact'	60–70 cm (24–28")
Asiatic Lily	*Lilium* 'Moulin Rouge'	1 M (3')
Asiatic Lily	*Lilium* 'Rhodos'	45 cm–1 M (1.5–3')
Asiatic Lily	*Lilium* 'Yellow Blaze'	1–1.3 M (3–4')
Daffodil	*Narcissus* 'Carlton'	45 cm (18")
Tulip	*Tulipa* 'Hytuna'	30 cm (12")
Tulip	*Tulipa* 'Orange Emperor'	45 cm (18")
Tulip	*Tulipa* 'Parade'	60 cm (24")
Shrubs and Vines		
Ville de Lyon Clematis	*Clematis* 'Ville de Lyon'	4 M (13')
Gold Twig Dogwood	*Cornus sericea* 'Flaviramea'	2 M (7')
Golden Broom	*Cytisus ratisbonensis*	1 M (3')
Dyer's Greenwood	*Genista tinctoria*	60 cm (24")
Potentilla	*Potentilla fruticosa*	1 M (3')
Goldfinger Potentilla	*Potentilla fruticosa* 'Goldfinger'	1 M (3')
Red Ace Potentilla	*Potentilla fruticosa* 'Red Ace'	1 M (3')
Golden Elder	*Sambucus racemosa* 'Plumosa Aurea'	2–3 M (7–10')
Gold Flame Spirea	*Spiraea* x *bumalda* 'Gold Flame'	1 M (3')

SPREAD	FLOWER COLOUR	COMMENTS
45 cm (18")	red	scented, attracts bees and butterflies
1 M (3')	red	long-lived double blooms
30–40 cm (12–16")	orange, yellow, pastels, white	satiny blooms, freely self-seeds
30–90 cm (12–36")	red	satiny blooms, hairy foliage
varies	pink, blue, purple, white	prefers well-drained soil
45–60 cm (18–24")	wide variety	excellent cut flower
1 M (3')	yellow	extended blooming, late season colour
1–1.5 M (3–5')	yellow, gold	excellent cut flower
25–50 cm (10–20")	orange, yellow	large buttercuplike blooms, tolerates partial shade
20–25 cm (8–10")	red	brilliant colour for shady borders and containers
varies	yellow	spring flowering, excellent for naturalizing
10–15 cm (4–6")	red	excellent cut flower
varies	yellow	heavily ruffled blooms, good accent
varies	yellow	clear yellow blooms, strong grower
varies	orange	blooms have purple brush marks
varies	red	strong grower, excellent cut flower
varies	red	large glossy red blooms
varies	yellow	excellent cut flower
varies	yellow	spring flowering, bright and showy
varies	yellow	spring flowering, double blooms
varies	orange	spring flowering, large long-lasting blooms
varies	red	spring flowering, good in backs of borders
2 M (7')	red	abundant red blooms
2 M (7')	white	gold and yellow stems
1 M (3')	yellow	abundant yellow blooms
1 M (3')	yellow	abundant yellow blooms
1 M (3')	wide variety	summer blooms
1 M (3')	yellow	attractive yellow blooms
1 M (3')	red	attractive red blooms
2–3 M (7–10')	white	golden yellow foliage
1 M (3')	pink	attractive yellow foliage

CHAPTER
13

GARDEN ACCENTS

"The sculptor does not work for the anatomist,
but for the common observer of life
and nature"
–John Ruskin

Garden ornaments have always played a significant role in garden design. The earliest gardens of Egypt, Rome and Greece featured statues from their pantheons of gods, goddesses, heroes and heroines. Colonnades were adorned with carefully crafted bronze and marble works that represented prevalent beliefs about humanity, nature and the cosmos.

Today, garden ornaments are used principally for decoration. They enrich the garden room by integrating the man-made into the natural environment. They create moods, invite discovery of the garden and otherwise add further touches of the gardenmaker's unique personality. Skillfully used, they can transform the ordinary into the extraordinary.

Birds are natural residents in the garden. In sculptural form, this crane represents long life.

To give your reproductions instant antiquity, try brushing them with a blended mixture of buttermilk, sphagnum moss and a little water.

SELECTING GARDEN ACCENTS

What qualifies as art in the garden is a purely personal affair. It may take the form of classical sculptures, urns or sundials that routinely depict themes from the arts and seasons. It may equally take the form of contemporary sculptures that represent nothing but their own beauty and grace. But the list doesn't end here. Many gardeners' tastes run to folk art ornaments such as interesting weather vanes, birdhouses and feeders that blend beauty with utility. For others, garden art is discovered in found objects such as stone or driftwood shaped by nature itself or in antique apple baskets, packing crates and rusted wheelbarrows originally designed for practical purposes.

Shopping for that ideal piece will require diligence. Garden boutiques and centres stock many high-quality reproductions of classical statuary as well as modestly priced cast-concrete urns and birdbaths. The well-healed gardener may turn to galleries as a source of contemporary sculpture, but those with a modest budget may find much value in the work of art students at a local college or art school. More determined treasure hunters may scour antique sales and stores in search of architectural fragments that add drama to their gardens. Even wreckers' yards and yard sales can yield objects awaiting only the gardener's imagination to transform them into art.

DESIGNING WITH GARDEN ACCENTS

The key to artfully integrating ornaments into your garden setting is to consider your garden's character. A small, formal urban setting may best lend itself to a reproduction of a classical sculpture, urn or sundial. A large informal garden, on the other hand, may best benefit from a touch of casual flair supplied by a contemporary piece of stone, metal, wood or concrete sculpture. A country garden may be the ideal location for unique yard animals forged of rusted railway spikes among drifts of wildflowers. The focal points often needed on a large acreage may be supplied by rusty ploughs and antique farm implements. The rural perennial garden can be made more aesthetically pleasing with pieces of driftwood.

Animals and birds are natural residents of gardens. In sculptural form, they often have a symbolic meaning. Cranes, for example, represent long life. They can be artfully used near a water garden or woodland area. A wide range of bird statuary, including doves, owls and even eagles, can also add ambiance to your garden. Whether you choose statuary resembling animals, characters from mythology or even somewhat sinister-looking gargoyles, these silent sentinels will add personality to your garden.

ESTABLISHING FOCAL POINTS AND BOUNDARIES

Garden accents can serve to draw attention to parts of the garden or establish transitions between them. When statuary or other ornaments are used in the centre of a formal garden, the whole design seems to radiate from that focal point. You can achieve this effect in a variety of ways. If your garden is large, you might create a carpet of colourful perennials or annuals radiating from the base of a large sundial or statue. For character and charm in the smaller garden, a smaller sundial or birdbath will achieve the same effect. Centrally located wooden frames or obelisks covered with flowering plants can also be used. It's important that the size and style of the piece be suited to your garden's character.

Garden accents can also establish multiple focal points within different areas of your garden. The monotony of a long stretch of uniformly shaped hedge or fence can suddenly be thrown into bold relief by introducing the contrasting lines of a piece of modern sculpture. To add solid grace to a formal entrance, consider the qualities of a complementary piece of classically styled sculpture. If your tastes run to the more exotic, explore the possibilities of a contrasting piece of contemporary art. A small plot of roses in a larger setting can suddenly be transformed into an attention-getting part of the garden by adding a skillfully placed piece of sculpture. Such a scene almost automatically suggests a traditionally styled statue because of the close association of roses

A trellis draped in vines is the perfect meeting of the manmade and the natural.

with romance and antiquity. But a contemporary abstract piece may do just as well. Distant vistas in the garden can suddenly spring to the viewer's attention when they are set off with a statue or ornament at the end of a path or walkway.

Statuary and ornaments can also serve to indicate boundaries between areas in the garden. Identical pieces of statuary on either side of a walkway can serve as focal points, but they also can define an entrance into another section of the garden and provide reason to pause and appreciate something botanically provocative. Decorative structures such as arbors can establish passageways between garden areas. Their trelliswork extends an invitation to colourful climbing vines such as clematis (*Clematis* spp.), dropmore scarlet trumpet honeysuckle (*Lonicera* x *brownii* 'Dropmore Scarlet Trumpet') or annual sweet peas (*Lathyrus odoratus*) that become galleries of sweet perfumes and secluded ambiance. A strategically placed arbor will draw the eye through the space, either diverting attention from an unpleasant view or enhancing a spectacular one. Arbor designs can be as simple as inexpensive prefabricated lattice spanning the posts on either side of a gate or as fancy as wrought iron grillwork with intricate patterns of decorative vines and flowers.

INVITING DISCOVERY

Not all displays of statuary or ornaments need be dramatic or even immediately visible to the viewer. Often, a small piece of art in the right place can be a delightful surprise for visitors to wander across. Small ornamental frogs, turtles and snails—either precast or paper mache lookalikes—invite further discovery when located near pathways or tucked between shrubbery. Small cherub figures will set the mood in a tranquil corner of a small garden. Locate them near ferns, hostas and lily-of-the-valley. A design emulating a woodland setting might benefit in a more subtle way through the careful integration of an old stump.

BIRDHOUSES AND FEEDERS

Garden ornaments can fulfill both utilitarian and decorative purposes. Of particular interest to many gardeners are birdhouses and feeders. Whether you choose examples resembling anything from a chateau to a local saloon, locate them near a favourite bench or other convenient observation point so you can thoroughly enjoy the joys of bird watching. Many garden centres and boutiques stock a tremendous variety of birdhouses and feeders in a wide range of styles and prices. Manufacturers' recommendations can help you choose the right house and location to attract the species you desire.

PERGOLAS AND GAZEBOS

Pergolas and gazebos extend living space into the garden. They provide places for quiet solitary contemplation as well as outdoor entertaining.

The basic design of the pergola has not changed since the time of the ancient Egyptians when it supported grapevines. Generally speaking, upright pillars support overhead wooden beams. The structural pillars can be made from a variety of materials—from solid wood to metal to masonry. They can be created different styles—from the ornate to the rustic—to complement the architecture of virtually any home. Clad their walls in vines and climbers, and position containers of colourful cascading annuals on their overhead beams.

Like pergolas, gazebos can reflect a variety of styles—from the elegance of an eight-sided Victorian replica to the rustic charm of a simpler four-sided country retreat. A gazebo tucked in the back corner of your garden offers privacy, a place to unwind and read a book or simply enjoy alfresco meals on warm summer days. Large overhead structures like gazebos and pergolas attract a great deal of attention, and so they need to be well anchored in a balanced garden design that includes plantings of trees or larger shrubs. For many gardeners, gazebos or pergolas represent the final element in the convergence of people and nature that is the goal of every garden designer.

Garden accents should provide year-round enjoyment. Besides creating moods and banishing sinister spirits during the growing season, well-chosen statuary or ornaments can add interest to the winter garden. When shrouded with fallen snow, statuary has a special aura of peacefulness all its own.

The quiet presence of this statue adds striking ambiance to this garden scene.

CHAPTER

14

LATIN LINGO

*"I love these beautiful and peaceful tribes
and wish I was better acquainted
with them"*

–W.S. Landor

Knowing a plant's botanical name is a first step in understanding it. From the beginning of time people have been organizing similar plants into groups. Plants were once grouped according to whether or not they had similar medicinal or herbal uses, but this primitive method of classification was confusing. In the early 1700s, Swedish botanist Carl Linnaeus developed the binomial system of classifying and naming plants that is still in use today. His two-word system, based on the plant's structural features, eliminated the confusion caused by the use of common plant names. While I would never suggest that we stop talking informally about pussytoes, windflowers or love-in-a-mist, Latin botanical names are understood internationally and so bypass the language and cultural barriers created by common names.

During Linnaeus' day, Latin was the written and spoken language of the educated. Under their direction botanical Latin became a richly descriptive language unto itself, incorporating words from Greek and other languages. When the appropriate word did not exist in Greek or Latin, a plant was often compared with animals, objects and even mythical goddesses— all in an effort to describe features and name the plant. It is little wonder that botanical names sound so poetic—reason enough to learn a bit more about them.

Let's take a walk through the flower garden and discover, through nomenclature, the history represented there. Almost every gardener is familiar with the colourful snapdragon and the warm shades of orange and yellow calendula. The showy snapdragons are botanically known as *Antirrhinum majus* and are members of the Figwort family. Calendula, a member of the daisy family, is botanically titled *Calendula officinalis*.

The first word of the binomial (or two-word) name, the *genus* (pl. *genera*), is usually a noun of Latin or Greek origin but always with a Latin ending. A genus contains scientifically similar plants and is always capitalized. The genus *Antirrhinum* is derived from the Greek *rhin*, meaning snout, for the unusual shape of the flowers. The genus *Calendula* is derived from the Latin *calendae* (the first day of the month), suggesting the long flowering period.

The second word of the binomial is technically called the *specific epithet*. It appears italicized in lower-case letters but may be capitalized if it is a person's name. The epithet is an adjective further describing the genus and giving clues about how it will behave in the garden. In the snapdragon, the specific epithet *majus* denotes the large size of the flowers. The epithet *officinalis* was applied to the calendula because at one time it was believed to have medicinal properties. A plant that is *compactus* or *nanus* will stay small. If *elatus* or *giganteus,* it will be unusually tall or large. If it is *admirabilis* or *elegans,* it may delight you. A flower that is *rubra* (or red) will not be suited for your all-white garden. You'll need to find flowers labelled *alba*. If fragrance is a virtue to you, then select *fragrans* or *odoratus*. Conversely, you might not like the unpleasant *graveolens* or *foetidus* in your garden.

The name of a species is a combination of the genus name and the specific epithet. A species is usually defined as a group of closely related plants within a genus. To ensure you get what you want when ordering from a nursery or seed company, use both names. Ordering a *Dianthus* alone, for instance, could bring any of approximately 300 different plants. If you ordered *Dianthus deltoides,* you'd receive a low-growing plant with tiny carmine-pink flowers. Had you ordered *Dianthus plumarius,* you would receive a still-charming pink flowering plant but with bigger flowers and entirely different foliage. But whatever you ordered, you would receive something heavenly because *Dianthus* is derived from *dios*, meaning of *Zeus*, and *anthos*, meaning flower—literally *flower of the gods.*

Of special interest to gardeners are the cultivated varieties, or *cultivars*, proliferated not by nature but by people. Cultivar names appear in plain (not italic) type and are enclosed in single quotation marks. For example, *Campanula carpatica* 'Blue Carpet' has showy blue flowers. Some cultivars will retain their distinguishing characteristics when reproduced sexually or asexually. Varieties defined by *var.* are naturally occurring rather than cultivated species.

Hybrids, which are produced by crossing any two genetically different parents, should be propagated asexually (that is, with plant tissue) as their seeds are often sterile, or they do not produce genetically identical plants. The multiplication sign x of *Delphinium* x *cultorum* denotes that it is of hybrid origin and is expressed as "the hybrid species" or "the hybrid genus" if the x appears before the genus.

As your skills develop and you discover the nuances of Latin lingo, your research may find a third element after the binomial name—the authority or abbreviated name of the scientist who named the species. In the example *Primula auricula* L., the L is the abbreviation for Carl Linnaeus. Many books, catalogues and journals routinely omit the authority for brevity and simplicity.

Though Latin binomial names are understood internationally, botanists are continually refining the art of plant classification, and new names are often assigned to familiar plants. The list of rules for naming plants found in the *International Code of Botanical Nomenclature* and the *International Code of Cultivated Plants* is extensive, exacting and continually evolving. Most recently, for example, the *Chrysanthemum* genus, containing the much-loved garden mums and daisies, was divided into 14 new genera. Only three species remain as true chrysanthemums. Approximately 40 species of these favourites adopted the new name *Dendranthema*. The well-known shasta daisy became *Leucanthemum*. It will take time for these changes in nomenclature to make their way into catalogues, garden centre literature and general usage. At the time of printing, the particular changes noted here are very recent, so for the reader's convenience, the former names have been retained.

Hortus Third is a widely recognized standard reference work that compiles cultivated plants for the United States and Canada. Though very expensive, it is an excellent guide for truly fanatic gardeners.

COMMONLY USED LATIN NAMES

Growth Habits
aerius – aerial (above ground)
adscendens – rising gradually
arboreus – treelike
aromaticus – aromatic (fragrant)
biennis – biennial (completing the life cycle in two growing seasons)
compacta – compact
elatus – tall
foetidus – bad smelling
fragrans – fragrant
giganteus – giant
nanus – dwarf or small
ordoratus – fragrant
patens – spreading
pendulus – hanging down
reptans – creeping
tomentosus – densely woolly

Colours
alba – white
amethystinus – violet
argenteus – silver
atropurpureus – deep magenta
aureus – gold
cardinalis – red
chrysanthus – gold
citrinus – yellow
flavus – pure yellow
glaucous – hazy grey
purpureus – purple
roseolus – pink
rubens – reddish
sanguineus – dark red

Geographic Descriptions
canadensis – Canada
australiensis – Australia
australis – southern
borealis – northern
californicus – California
chinensis or *sinensis* – China
chilensis – Chile
montanus – mountain
japonica – Japan
sibirica – Siberia
alpinus – mountain
americanus – America
britannicus – Great Britain

SUGGESTED READING

Throughout the years, I've counted myself lucky to have had the sage advice of many fine gardeners through their books. Here are a few that show their status in my library by their wear. Some may be out of print but still available in libraries. Others may have reemerged in new or reprinted editions.

Beales, Peter. *Roses: An Illustrated Encyclopaedia and Grower's Handbook of Species Roses, Old Roses and Modern Roses, Shrub Roses and Climbers.* New York: Henry Holt, 1992.

Berral, Julia S. *The Garden: An Illustrated History.* New York: Viking, 1966.

Coates, Alice M. *Garden Shrubs and their Histories.* New York: Simon and Schuster, 1992.

Cormack, R.G.H. *Wild Flowers of Alberta.* Edmonton: Hurtig, 1977.

Jekyll, Gertrude. *Colour Schemes for the Flower Garden.* Woodbridge, England: Antique Collectors' Club, 1982.

Knowles, Hugh. *Woody Ornamentals for the Prairies.* Edmonton: University of Alberta Press, 1989.

Moss, E.H. *Flora of Alberta.* Toronto: University of Toronto Press, 1983.

Osborne, Robert. *Roses for Canadian Gardens.* Toronto: Key Porter, 1991.

Paterson, Allen. *Plants for Shade and Woodland.* Toronto: Fitzhenry and Whiteside, 1987.

Shewchuk, George W. *Rose Gardening on the Prairies.* Edmonton: University of Alberta Press, 1988.

Staff of the L.H. Bailey Hortium. *Hortus Third.* New York: Macmillan, 1976.

Stern, William T. *Botanical Latin.* Vermont: David and Charles, 1983.

Toop, Edgar W. and Sara Williams. *Perennials for the Prairies.* Edmonton: University of Alberta Press, 1991.

Verey, Rosemary. *The Flower Arranger's Garden.* Toronto: Stoddart, 1989.

PLANT NAME INDEX

Annuals

Ageratum houstonianum 'Blue Blazer' (ageratum), 133, 144
Ageratum houstonianum 'Fairy Pink' (ageratum), 148
Ageratum houstonianum 'Hawaii White' (ageratum), 152
Antirrhinum majus (snapdragon), 58, 68, 70
Antirrhinum majus 'Carousel' (snapdragon), 156
Antirrhinum majus 'Liberty Red' (snapdragon), 156
Antirrhinum majus 'Sonnet Pink' (snapdragon), 148
Antirrhinum majus 'Tahiti White' (snapdragon), 138, 152

Begonia x *semerflorens cultorum* (fibrous begonia), 124
Begonia x *tuberhybrida* (tuberous begonia),124
Brachycome iberidifolia (Swan River daisy), 144, 148, 152
Brassica oleracea (ornamental kale), 124
Browallia speciosa (browallia), 124
Browallia speciosa 'Marine Bells' (browallia), 133, 144
Browallia speciosa 'Silver Bells' (browallia), 152

Calendula officinalis (calendula), 53, 58, 68, 70, 100, 143
Calendula officinalis 'Cream Beauty' (calendula), 152
Calendula officinalis 'Pacific Beauty' (calendula), 156
China aster *Callistephus chinensis*, 70
Callistephus chinensis 'Milady' series (China aster), 156
Callistephus chinensis 'Milady Blue' (China aster), 133, 144
Callistephus chinensis 'Milady Rose' (China aster), 148
Callistephus chinensis 'Milady White' (China aster), 152
Celosia argentea var. *cristata* (celosia), 68, 70
Chrysanthemum morifolium (chrysanthemum), 70
Clarkia amoena (clarkia), 68, 70
Clarkia elegans 'Royal Banquet Mix' (clarkia), 135, 148, 156
Cordyline indivisa (dracena), 124
Cosmos bipinnatus (cosmos), 68, 70, 135, 148
Cosmos bipinnatus 'White Sonata' (cosmos), 152
Cosmos sulphureus 'Sunny Red' (cosmos), 156
Crepis rubra 'Rosea' (crepis), 135, 148
Cymbalaria spp. (Kennelworth ivy), 120, 124

Dahlia pinnata (annual dahlia), 68, 70, 148
Delphinium spp. (larkspur), 68, 70
dusty miller, 70

Exacum affine (Persian violet), 100

Fuchsia spp. (fuchsia), 120, 124

Helianthus annus (sunflower), 53, 58
Helichrysum spp. (strawflower), 68, 70
Heliotrope arborescens (heliotrope), 100

Iberis 'Giant White Hyacinth' (annual candytuft), 152
Iberis spp. (annual candytuft), 133, 144
Iberis umbellata (annual candytuft), 135, 148
Impatiens wallerana (impatiens), 120, 124
Ipomoea 'Heavenly Blue' (morning glory), 133, 144

Lathyrus odoratus (sweet pea), 53, 68, 99, 100, 148, 152, 163
Lathyrus odoratus 'Bijou' (dwarf sweet pea), 55, 58
Lathyrus odoratus 'Knee-Hi' (dwarf sweet pea), 55, 58, 70, 100, 144
Lathyrus odoratus 'Little Sweetheart' (dwarf sweet pea), 55, 58
Lathyrus odoratus 'Spencer Mix' (tall sweet pea), 55, 58, 70, 100, 133, 144
Lathyrus odoratus 'Winston Churchill' (sweet pea), 156
Lavatera trimestris (lavatera), 68, 70
Lavatera trimestris 'Mont Blanc' (lavatera), 138, 152
Lavatera trimestris 'Silver Cup' (lavatera), 135, 148
Limonium sinuatum (annual statice), 70
Lobelia erinus (lobelia), 78, 124
Lobelia erinus 'Colour Cascade Mixture' (lobelia), 156
Lobelia erinus 'Crystal Palace' (lobelia), 133, 144
Lobelia erinus 'Rosamond' (lobelia), 148
Lobelia erinus 'White Lady' (lobelia), 138, 152
Lobularia maritima (sweet alyssum), 53, 58, 99, 100
Lobularia maritima 'Carpet of Snow', 138, 152
Lobularia maritima 'Royal Carpet' (sweet alyssum), 144
Lobularia maritima 'Wonderland' (sweet alyssum), 148
Lunaria annua (money plant), 68, 70

Matthiola incana (stocks), 68, 70, 100
Matthiola incana 'Cinderella' series (stocks), 156
Matthiola incana 'Cinderella White' (stocks), 152
Matthiola incana 'Midget Rose' (stocks), 148
Matthiola longipetala (evening scented stocks), 98, 100, 138, 152
Mirabilis jalapa (four-o'clocks), 100
Miscanthus sinensis 'Silberfeder' (silver feather grass), 70
Monarda citriodora (lemon bee balm), 100

Nemophila menziesii (baby-blue-eyes), 144
Nicotiana affinis (evening scented nicotiana), 98
Nicotiana alata (nicotiana), 100, 124
Nicotiana 'Domino Picotee' (nicotiana), 148
Nicotiana spp. (nicotiana), 70, 98, 100
Nicotiana 'Starship' series (nicotiana), 156
Nicotiana 'White Bedder' (nicotiana), 138, 152
Nigella spp. (love-in-a-mist), 68, 70

Oenothera odorata (evening primrose), 98, 100

Papaver commutatum 'Ladybird' (Ladybird poppy), 156
Pelargonium graveolens (scented geranium), 99, 100
Pelargonium peltatum (ivy geranium), 124
Pelargonium peltatum 'Belladonna' (ivy geranium), 148
Pelargonium peltatum 'Double Lilac White' (ivy geranium), 152
Pelargonium peltatum 'Summer Showers' series (ivy geranium), 156
Pelargonium x *domesticum* (Martha Washington geranium), 120, 124
Pelargonium x *domesticum* 'Crystal' (Martha Washington geranium), 152
Pelargonium x *domesticum* 'Royalty' series (Martha Washington geranium), 156
Pelargonium x *domesticum* 'Vavra Josy' (Martha Washington geranium), 148
Pelargonium x *hortorum* 'Alba' (zonal geranium), 138, 152
Pelargonium x *hortorum* 'Kim' (zonal geranium), 156
Pelargonium x *hortorum* 'Pink Expectations' (zonal geranium), 148
Pennisetum alopecuriodes (fountain grass), 70
Petunia x *hybrida* (petunia), 41, 98, 99, 100
Petunia x *hybrida* 'Blue Daddy' (petunia), 133, 144
Petunia x *hybrida* 'Calypso' (petunia), 156
Petunia x *hybrida* 'Pink Daddy' (petunia), 135, 148
Petunia x *hybrida* 'White Cascade' (petunia), 138, 152
Portulaca grandiflora (portulaca), 53, 58
Portulaca grandiflora 'Sundance Mix' (portulaca), 156
Portulaca grandiflora 'Sundial Fuchsia' (portulaca), 148
Portulaca grandiflora 'Sundial White' (portulaca), 152

Salpiglossis sinuata (painted tongue), 68, 70, 156
Salvia coccinea 'Lady in Red' (salvia), 156
Salvia farinacea 'Victoria Blue' (salvia), 133, 144
Salvia splendens 'Empire White' (salvia), 152
Salvia splendens 'Melba' (salvia), 148
Schizanthus x *wisetonensis* (butterfly flower), 70, 124

Tagetes erecta 'Excel Primrose' (African marigold), 156
Tagetes patula 'Early Spice Saffron' (French marigold), 156
Tagetes spp. (marigold), 53, 58, 70
Tropaeolum majus (nasturtium), 41, 52, 59, 99, 100, 143
Tropaeolum majus 'Whirlybird' (nasturtium), 156

Verbena x *hybrida* 'Delight' (verbena), 148
Verbena x *hybrida* 'Blue Lagoon' (verbena), 133, 144
Verbena x *hybrida* 'Novalis White' (verbena), 152
Verbena x *hybrida* 'Peaches and Cream' (verbena), 156
Viola spp. (pansy), 53, 58, 68, 120, 124
Viola 'Universal Yellow' (pansy), 156
Viola x *wittrockiana* 'Crystal Bowl White' (pansy), 138, 152
Viola x *wittrockiana* 'Imperial Frosty Rose' (pansy), 135, 148
Viola x *wittrockiana* 'Silver Wings' (pansy), 133, 144

Zinnia elegans (zinnia), 53, 58, 70
Zinnia elegans 'Rose Pinwheel' (zinnia), 148
Zinnia elegans 'Star White' (zinnia), 152
Zinnia erecta 'Paintbrush' (zinnia), 156
Zinnia erecta 'Scarlet Splendor' (zinnia), 156

Bulbs and Others

Allium caeruleum (blue globe onion), 46, 72, 114, 146
Allium ostrowskianum (Ostrowsky onion), 46, 114

Begonia x *tuberhybrida* (tuberous begonia), 72, 120, 143
Begonia x *tuberhybrida* 'Allan Langdon' (tuberous begonia), 158
Begonia x *tuberhybrida* 'Billy Langdon' (tuberous begonia), 154
Begonia x *tuberhybrida* 'Nonstop Pink' (tuberous begonia), 150

Chionodoxa gigantea (glory-of-the-snow), 154
Chionodoxa lucilliae (glory-of-the-snow), 46, 132, 146
Chionodoxa lucilliae 'Rosea' (glory-of-the-snow), 150
Chionodoxa spp. (glory-of-the-snow), 114
Colchicum spp. (autumn crocus), 114
Crocus chrysanthus 'Zwanenburg Bronze' (crocus), 158
Crocus 'Joan of Arc' (crocus), 154
Crocus 'Queen of the Blues' (crocus), 146
Crocus 'Ruby Giant' (crocus), 150
Crocus spp. (crocus), 46, 96, 100, 114

Fritillaria pallidiflora (fritillaria), 41, 46, 72, 114

Galanthus nivalis (snowdrop), 154
Gladiolus 'Fire Engine' (gladioli), 158
Gladiolus 'Great River' (gladioli), 146
Gladiolus 'Rookie' (gladioli), 150
Gladiolus spp. (gladioli), 63, 72
Gladiolus 'White Prosperity' (gladioli), 154

Iris danfordiae (danfordiae iris), 46, 114
Iris reticulata (early spring iris), 40, 46, 110, 114, 132, 146
Iris x *germanica* (bearded iris), 42–43, 46, 72, 100, 114, 132
Iris x *germanica* 'Babbling Brook' (bearded iris), 132, 146
Iris x *germanica* 'Beverly Sills' (bearded iris), 150
Iris x *germanica* 'Honky Tonk Blues' (bearded iris), 132, 146
Iris x *germanica* 'Immortality' (bearded iris), 154
Iris x *germanica* 'Lemon Mist' (bearded iris), 158
Iris x *germanica* 'Memphis Blues' (bearded iris), 132, 146
Iris x *germanica* 'Sapphire Hills' (bearded iris), 132, 146

Lilium 'Connecticut King' (Asiatic lily), 139, 158
Lilium 'Corsica' (Asiatic lily), 134, 150
Lilium 'Crete' (Asiatic lily), 134, 150
Lilium 'Impact' (Asiatic lily), 139, 158
Lilium 'Malta' (Asiatic lily), 134, 150
Lilium 'Moulin Rouge' (Asiatic lily), 139, 158
Lilium 'Polka Dot' (Asiatic lily), 134, 150
Lilium 'Rhodos' (Asiatic lily), 139, 158
Lilium 'Roma' (Asiatic lily), 154
Lilium spp. (Asiatic lily), 68, 72, 77, 100, 114, 134
Lilium 'Yellow Blaze' (Asiatic lily), 139, 158

Muscari armeniacum (grape hyacinth), 41, 46
Muscari armeniacum 'Blue Spike' (grape hyacinth), 132, 146
Muscari botryoides (grape hyacinth), 41, 46, 110
Muscari botryoides 'Album' (grape hyacinth), 154
Muscari spp. (grape hyacinth), 100, 114, 139

Narcissus 'Carlton' (daffodil), 158
Narcissus 'Mount Hood' (daffodil), 154
Narcissus spp. (daffodil), 46, 66, 72, 96, 100, 114

Puschkinia scilloides var. *libanotica* (puschkinia), 132, 146
Puschkinia scilloides var. *libanotica* 'Alba' (puschkinia), 154

Scilla sibirica (Siberian squill), 41, 46
Scilla sibirica 'Alba' (squill), 154
Scilla sibirica 'Spring Beauty' (squill), 132, 146
Scilla spp. (squill), 46, 110, 114

Tulipa 'Burgundy Lace' (tulip), 41, 48
Tulipa 'Diana' (tulip), 42, 48, 137, 154
Tulipa 'Fancy Frills' (tulip), 42, 48
Tulipa 'Fringed Rhapsody' (tulip), 41, 48
Tulipa 'Hamilton' (tulip), 42, 48

SUBJECT NAME INDEX